healer —
essence — back
article
art healing

at
re...
emotional spiritual

SACRED
NECESSITIES

alexis (alexus)

self love   autonomy   in love
                            ganish
                         ⑥

insights — ganish
agitates confidence —   ⑧
                          week

schere
life

SACRED
Necessities

gifts for living with
passion, purpose, and grace

TERRY HERSHEY

Sorin Books Notre Dame, Indiana

For Zach

On page 15, "Gift" is from *The Collected Poems 1931-1987*, by Czeslaw Milosz
Copyright © 1988 by Czeslaw Milosz Royalties, Inc.
Reprinted by permission of HarperCollins Publishers
On page 166 the twelve lines are from "Will you be my friend", pp. 90-92, from *Will You Be My Friend?* by James Kavanaugh
Copyright © 1971, 1984 by James Kavanaugh; Illustrations copyright © 1984 by Marjorie Luy
Reprinted by permission of HarperCollins Publishers
"Will" is copyright ©1996 by Marcia Lee Falk. Excerpted from *The Book of Blessings: New Jewish Prayers for Daily Life, the Sabbath, and the New Moon Festival* by Marcia Falk (Harper, 1996; paperback edition, Beacon Press, 1999). Used by permission of the author.

www.sorinbooks.com
International Standard Book Number: 1-893732-93-2
Cover and text design by David R. Scholtes
Printed and bound in the United States of America.
Library of Congress Cataloging-in-Publication Data is available.

Contents

"So the gods shake us from our sleep."

—Mary Oliver

"What grace to be alive and know the

day in all its sweetness!"

—Ram Dass

A Note to the Reader

Is this book for you?

It is a book for people who love life.

And for people who wish to love life, but who are temporarily stymied.

Captives to busyness, disappointment, exhaustion, anger, apathy, an excess of caution, or even a good reputation, we carry around an unused life—as if life is a savings bond to be withdrawn only when mandatory.

Instead of living, we are star-struck. In a world of celebrities, we live vicariously through people who "have it all," those who grace the beguiling covers of supermarket magazines. It goes against our better judgment, but there is something fundamentally comforting about betting our emotional nest egg on a winner.

Although, truth be told, it is people who are alive in their own skin who stand out.

Or choose another description: to be centered, balanced, passionate, authentic, purposeful, or alive in our own skin. These all point us in the same direction: to people who practice a few sacred necessities. Practice that opens the heart and rekindles the spirit. And in this case, practice is everything. Theory is for folks with too much time on their hands, and a heavy dose of Puritan guilt, leaving them with the notion that it is better to play the right notes than to hear the music.

We think of living a good life as some kind of western birthright. Such thinking becomes toxic when it is fueled by three thousand advertisements every single day telling us what to buy, or more realistically, what to feel guilty about, as if somehow we have missed the boat to success. It is a cultural full-court press about what it means to be human, and we live in perpetual consternation over completing some list of expectations, always wondering if we measure up. In our fixation to find the answers, we miss . . .

. . . the small gifts of life,

. . . the serendipitous gifts of grace,

. . . the presence of the holy,

. . . and the gentle doses of the sacred reflected in our everyday—and extraordinarily ordinary—world.

It is true. We don't fear death. As Rabbi Harold Kushner reminds us, what we fear is coming to the end of our lives and realizing that we never lived. And somewhere on the way to happiness or inner peace, it hits us that we are looking too hard for what we already hold, but have not yet embraced.

> "Why do we have all these feelings, dreams, and hopes if we don't ever use them? That's where Shirley Valentine disappoints. She got lost in all this unused life. I've fallen in love with the idea of living."
>
> —From the movie *Shirley Valentine*

On a cross-country flight I am accosted by an overzealous pyramid marketer. He does not introduce himself as a pyramid marketer. He simply smiles, like he knows me from somewhere, and says, "Hi, I'm David, may I ask you a question?"

At this point, I still believe it necessary to be polite. As a Midwestern boy, polite is my built-in default mode, my emotional autopilot. "Fire away," I tell him.

"Do you want your life to be successful?" he asks, earnestly, without a hint of irony in his voice.

I look into his eyes, waiting to see if there is a punch line. I feel like I'm in a foreign film and there is a lag in the translation. I wonder what kind of person answers, "No, but thank you for asking. In fact, I want my life to be one of unmitigated failure. I hope to be the poster boy for unparalleled mediocrity."

He is still watching me, waiting for my answer. I decide that my insight is best kept to myself, so I nod halfheartedly.

"I thought so," he tells me, like a teacher affirming my correct answer. He leans closer, "Would you like to earn more money than you are earning now? And what if I were to tell you that it is easy to do?"

A part of me is still looking for the hidden camera. Another part of me is curious about his pitch. This equation for life certainly is not unfamiliar, you know, a personalized life management system with an appropriate name: perhaps Vision Quest, or Beauty Vision, or even Mountaintop Living. In this equation Success = Money = the Good Life.

"Let me show you how you can have it all," he tells me, opening a three-ring binder with diagrams and glossy photos.

"This is a life to befit a man of your stature," he adds, playing the butter-up-the-middle-aged-man card.

None of what he shows me is new. "Do you want the life of your dreams? Extra income? A second house? Vacations in the Caribbean?" He's flipping through the photos. One features a family on a white sand beach, the water a crystalline teal. The man, his wife, and two children are playing (or posing, I couldn't tell), apparently enjoying their newfound wealth. They each have loads of beautiful white teeth (and I wonder about the correlation). The photos are evocative and convincing, meant to make my own life feel pale or shallow or wanting in some way. It is important that I buy into the notion that this family has received the handbook about the fullness of life, while mine apparently was lost in the mail.

Even for all my moral-high-road skepticism, it's easy to be swayed by the scent of wealth. Especially when there are colored photographs. And all those beautiful white teeth!

He handed me his business card (with "find the life of your dreams!" embossed). I returned to reading my book, but my attention was drawn to the scene outside my window. We flew west toward Seattle, Beethoven's Ninth Symphony (in my earphones) resounding in my head. Mount Hood, Mount St. Helens, and Mount Rainer form a perfect trifecta in sharp relief in the dusk light. A capillary of metal gray clouds hung suspended above the peaks. The Cascade mountain range was powdered with snow, its valleys filled with clouds and fog now settled for the night. The serenity of the scene distracted me from the vexation brought on by the glamorous photographs.

My conversation with the young man selling the successful life unsettled me. So I spent an afternoon in a bookstore, jotting down the titles of the books displayed at a special self-help table.

There are ninety-nine ways to simplify my life, six fundamentals of success, a proven program for self-esteem, seven things happy couples do, and—if I had a good deal of time—one thousand two hundred inspiring ideas for happiness. I could change my life in thirty days, make twenty choices to transform my life, or visualize a new me in only seven days. But my favorite was: Eat chocolate naked and one hundred and forty-two other ways to attract attention and spark romance. This seemed to get to the heart of the matter.

I make no judgment about these books, but it confirmed what I already knew. There is no shortage of handbooks. And you've got to wonder about this bombardment of advice. It feels like Las Vegas, where the senses are over saturated, like a triple espresso caffeine hit to the cortex, an invigorating rush, pretty in its own way, but short-circuiting any objectivity.

We know we live in a world of self-improvement. That isn't news. Not that improvement in itself is a bad goal, but why must every event, circumstance, relationship, or exchange be evaluated on its ability to enhance quality? I have a similar reaction when people ask me about my career path. I make some joke about coming to two paths in the woods, taking the one less traveled and being lost in the woods ever since. And they give me the look reserved for adolescents who should be on medication. But then I don't believe that every event in my life must be a building block for life as it should be.

I've been asked—too often—what I believe. My favorite variation is any inquiry about my "doctrinal statement." This begins a volley of theological catch phrases, which have become *de facto* passwords for many religious organizations and communities. It's the way we tell who's "in" and who's "out." Passing muster in any doctrinal inquisition is an occupational hazard for those of us who rub shoulders with fervent religious folk—people who find serenity in doctrinal purity and have, from what I can tell, left the fiber out their diet.

Here's the odd part. I have never once been asked about what nourishes my soul. Or to list what moves me. Or for stories about what warms my blood, sends gooseflesh up my arms, makes me want to dance, makes me love life, or laugh and cry at the same time. I've been asked about what is appropriate, but never about what is important.

Truth is, there are only a few things that really matter, and those few things—those sacred necessities—matter immeasurably. Which means that if you are in a hurry for answers, this book may play havoc with your blood pressure and any need for order. Which is another way of saying that it might be good for what ails you.

> **"For the past eighty years I have started each day in the same manner. I go to the piano, and I play two preludes and fugues**

of Bach. It is sort of a benediction on the
house. But that is not its only meaning.
It is a rediscovery of the world in which
I have the joy of being a part. It fills me
with awareness of the wonder of life, with
a feeling of the incredible marvel of being
human. The music is never the same for
me, never. Each day it is something new,
fantastic and unbelievable."

—Pablo Casals (at age 93)

I love the book by a man who wrote about fly-fishing, stories about solitude and times with friends on rivers throughout the western states. Stories about listening, learning, awareness, reflection, questions, and small voices that speak to the heart. During his writing he was asked, "What is the purpose of your book?"

He paused, and answered, "I'm not sure, but it's a little too late for that now."

I can tell you this: These necessities—practices, ingredients—are sacred because they allow us to embrace the day, our life—this life—in all its fullness, with its disparities, its quirkiness, its demands, its unfairness, and its wondrous serendipities. These necessities are sacred because they do not lodge themselves on the surface of life. They enter into it, giving life its spice, its flavor, its fullness, its richness, its punch, and its power. Sacred necessities . . .

. . . enrich and develop our humanity,

. . . draw from the well of wonder and not just reason,

. . . help us to recover what may have been lost along the way.

When Patch Adams enrolled in medical school, the dean of students told him: "We are here to train the humanity out of you and make you something better. We're going to make you a doctor." It's the dilemma of our time: Do we choose to be human and authentic, or do we settle for a good reputation?

There are seven sacred necessities in this book. I chose seven for no particular reason. Although if it would ease anyone's mind, I could make up a reason. The number of necessities is not nearly as important as the fact that they are sacred. I meant to write eight necessities, but ran out of time. Truth be told, if my deadline was not looming, there could have been ten.

Which reminds me, I write the same way that I tour my garden each morning, following any scent or sight or sound. I seldom end up where I mean to go. I meander, following a train of thought where it takes me. I find that it helps if I look at an issue from every direction. If you come to my island, I'll take you for a walk in my garden, and we'll let the afternoon melt around us. And you will see that in the garden, each light—the soft light of early morning or the lavender light of late afternoon—gives a fresh or new sensation.

Read the book straight through if you wish. Or feel free to choose a more ambling pace. Read the chapters like mini-reflections, digesting truths slowly. You will read stories, musings, and reflections, and I'll borrow words of wisdom from many different traditions. Stories are important as they fill a container for our longings, anxieties, hopes, and dreams.

My son enters my study.

"What are you doing, dad?"

"Writing a book."

"What's your book about, dad?"

"It's called sacred necessities for people who love life."

"Oh." he is silent, his little brow thoughtfully furrowed, pondering the title. "Will it be a good book?"

He makes me smile. "I hope so," I tell him. "But you know what? Dad is having fun writing it."

> **A day so happy.**
> **Fog lifted early, I walked in the garden.**
> **Hummingbirds were stopping over**
> **   honeysuckle flowers.**
> **There was nothing on earth I wanted to**
> **   possess.**
> **I knew no one worth envying.**
> **Whatever evil I had suffered, I forgot.**
> **To think that once I was the same man**
> **   did not embarrass me.**
> **In my body I felt no pain.**
> **When straightening up, I saw the blue sea**
> **   and sails.**
>
> **—Czeslaw Milosz**

Learning the Big Leaf Dance

"We live like ill-taught piano students.

We're so inculcated with the flub that gets

us in dutch, we don't hear the music, we

only play the right notes."

—Robert Capon

My son Zachary loves to dance. As soon as he learned to walk, he began to dance. He would spin and hop and slap his feet on our hardwood floor. Beethoven or the Beatles, he's not picky about the music. Now almost seven, with his arms in the air, he looks like a cross between a Pentecostal revival preacher and a Native American shaman. His air of abandon is palpable.

This past autumn brought a remarkable gift to our island here in the Pacific Northwest—an October with almost no rainfall. October weather that not one old-time island resident could recall. It meant pleasant daytime temperatures, dry leaves crackling under foot, and cool, clear evenings.

Our deciduous trees do not have the vivid and oft-photographed autumn colors of the sugar maples of the East Coast. But we do have Acer macrophyllum or big leaf maples. Big leaf maple is the actual name; and it fits, as a single leaf can span fourteen inches. Each leaf looks as if it has been manufactured for effect, enlarged for classroom demonstration or to accommodate middle-aged eyesight. In autumn color, they stay true to their northwest sensibility and offer, shall we say, an understated palate ranging from Dijon mustard to a weathered barn-red.

Zachary has created his own big leaf dance. With a maple leaf in each hand, each looking like a giant fan, he gallops, skips, and hops in a circle, chanting. After a few minutes, he interrupts his dance to remind us that this is not a dance to be performed solitarily. He begins his instructions, "Okay everyone, this is the leaf dance, get your leaves ready. This is how you do it." For Zachary, leaf dances are a communal event, and he insists that his mother and father join him. I can tell you that this is not a dance for anyone squeamish about public opinion. Any onlooker would have wondered, snickered, and in all likelihood called for a sobriety test. Which may be appropriate. I know now that big leaf dancing can be intoxicating.

This is the measuring stick for all sacred necessities: they allow us to hear the music.

Asking the right questions

I've been subjected to many a hell-fire sermon. They were standard fare at the First Baptist Church of Colon, Michigan, the church of my boyhood, where I sat upright, obedient—third pew, left side. Every Sunday. No exceptions. Missing church carried an eternal penalty. I remember the pastor used to say frequently, "Christians who attend Sunday morning service love the church; Christians who attend Sunday night service love the pastor; but Christians who attend Sunday morning, Sunday night, and Wednesday night prayer service love God." (He was not a balanced man.) The subject matter of these sermons may have varied slightly, but the intent was always the same: to give us the good news, which was always some variation on the theme of spending eternity in hell. I never quite understood, even as a young boy, how this could be construed to be good news. But it sure made one wonder about the bad news. There is no doubt that these were sermons meant to fuel the fire of penance, since a guilty audience is always a rapt one, eager for any opportunity to make amends. Preachers—at least to me—seemed to enjoy rubbing it in our faces that not one of us was as far along as we thought.

I remember a funeral for two teenagers who died in a tragic auto accident. They were my age. They were friends of mine. There is no getting around a tragedy like that—one of life's capricious moments. Our knee-jerk need to make some sense of it all is understandable. There were many eulogies that day. Most of them were disguised as sermons with some imperative to find a moral lesson. One eulogist talked about my friends "burning themselves out for God." Both ends of the candle and all that. These sermons were meant to comfort us, to let us know that these young people didn't die in vain. But to seal the deal, we (those in attendance) were urged to swear off trivial pursuits in favor of commitments—and lives—that would make God proud.

The message was not lost on me, to be sure. Don't waste your life.

This is a seductive command to an impressionable kid. Because I knew in the core of my being that I had not done enough, that I had not been committed enough, and that I did not have enough faith. Doing the math in my head, I had, in fact, been wasting my life. These eulogizers wanted me to believe that every moment of my life was to be weighed instead of celebrated. Each day was to be evaluated instead of embraced. Each choice was to be judged instead of owned. And I left the service chastened, determined to live my life for God. That I had made this promise countless times before seemed unimportant, lost in my preoccupation with keeping score.

What I remember now, in retrospect, is that there were no eulogies about laughter, playing baseball, or weeks at summer camp spent by the lake. There were no stories about music or poetry, or unanswered questions, or moments of doubt or embarrassment.

And there were no eulogies about big leaf dancing.

There is an education—a way of learning about life—that assures us we will play the right notes. But there is another way. We learn to ask the right questions. We pay attention to the voices that teach us how to hear, play, and dance to the music.

In remembering the funeral of my friends, it seems that the adults asked the wrong questions. (It's a variation on a theme in *The Little Prince*: adults are people fueled by the need for data, information, and numbers.) And so we did not ask the important questions: "What music did your friends dance to? What poems made them cry or smile? What did their laughter sound like? What would light up their face?" Instead, we asked: "How old were they? What did they do? How did they earn money? How did they die? Was their life important?"

It is the same if you want to learn about me. My resume doesn't really help, unless we're discussing parental pride or some kind of bragging rights for a vocational turf war. It is not enough to say that I am fond of reading, addicted to golf, a reclusive gardener mostly at home ambling among perennials and roses, or that I served such and such parish in church ministry. They are all true facts about me, but not the whole story. I would need to tell you about the time I was unraveled by an iris. Or about the time my heart stopped, watching a bald eagle soar only a few feet above me head. Or the sheer delight of listening to my son sing and dance to the Beatles' "All You Need is Love."

Given the choice, I choose to see life a bit catawampus. Life is not about the right notes. It's about recovering the questions that allow us to hear the music. A father is concerned about his son's education at the new public school. They are a "back woods" family, far away from civilization and without any formal education. Still the father wonders about this new school and its curriculum. "What will they learn you?" he asks his son, "Will they learn you why the river makes that singing sound when the moon is right?" The poet Mary Oliver takes it a step further in her poem:

> **What did you notice?**
> **What did you hear?**
> **What did you admire?**
> **What astonished you?**
> **What would you like to see again?**

What was most tender?

What was most wonderful?

What did you think was happening?

Try these questions tonight for dinnertime conversation. You'll get that look. But it still beats, "How was work?" or "What did you do today?" Your family will take notice.

At the rabbit happy hour

When I lived in southern California, I spent three days a month at St. Andrew's Abbey, a Benedictine monastery in the high desert. It is in the proverbial middle-of-nowhere. I discovered quickly that the most difficult part of my routine involved filling the time. This is ironic for someone who complains about never having enough time and enlightening for a culture that views empty time as a threat, a void that needs to be filled.

Rabbit happy hour was my favorite time of day. Congregating off the patio near room number eleven, the rabbits threw a "ya'll come" neighborhood fiesta every night before dusk, so far as I could tell. They loitered and gossiped, nibbling on the small amounts of vegetation near the guest rooms. Beyond my room were miles of desert, a pin cushion punctured with Joshua trees and yucca plants stretching to the mountains. I would sit in my patio chair and watch the rabbits party.

I savored the time. It did not take long for my body, my mind, and my soul to mold itself to this new pace.

The difficulty came in trying to shake my inclination to do a day's end evaluation, to ascribe some value to my hour of rabbit-watching. What exactly does one use as a measuring stick for this odd spiritual discipline? I would sit with paper and pencil in hand, forcing myself to journal, to give meaning, as my mind wandered.

"So what did you do out there on your spiritual retreat?" I remember being asked by well meaning friends and loved ones. "Were you productive? (Did you fill your time the right way? Did you use your time wisely?)"

"I watched rabbits," I would tell them.

Their eyes would narrow, knowing my personality, knowing that surely I jested.

"No, really," I would say.

"But how do you justify that?" they would ask.

It's not an easy demon to exorcise, this need to list our feats. It takes a toll. Listen to *The Little Prince*,

> **I know a planet where there is a certain red-faced gentleman. He has never smelled a flower. He has never looked at a star. He has never loved anyone. He has never done anything in his life but add up figures. And all day he says over and over, just like you: "I am busy with matters of consequence!" And that makes him swell up with pride. But he is not a man—he is a mushroom.**

It's not just the pell-mell pacing. We are all aware that hectic and frantic comes with the turf. What ties us into knots is the implication that such a pace implies importance—that people who have Day-Timers full of appointments, reminders, and checklists deserve our jealousy and admiration. It all seems linked to some primitive fear of what we will become without that full schedule and the requisite array of distractions. What will we have to call on for affirmation? Will we be admired or ridiculed?

On the flip side, there is the implication that wasting time is the worst possible indictment about our personhood. I have a friend whose father would frequently interrogate her, "So, what are you going to do about that five minutes you just lost?"

This all runs pretty deep.

Patricia Raybon relates this memory from her own childhood in her book, *My First White Friend*:

> "Daddy's coming!"
>
> Two words shouldn't make the heart leap.
>
> But I always stood, straight up, from the
> jolt. Ready to, what?— flee, fight, blurt out
> some pathetic defense for whatever wrong
> thing I was doing at the moment. Especially
> if it was fun or lazy or silly. If it was TV
> or fast music or twisty dancing or finger
> snapping.
>
> His stern look, scrutinizing, upbraided me,
> a look that, in truth, probably said more

about the world outside than the life inside
our home. To deflect it, I'd grab a book, a
broom, a dust rag, a dishrag—any sure sign
of industry, or productivity. That would
make me OK, for now. But just *being* there—
it didn't seem to be enough.

Just being. How did this become such an
ordeal?

Isn't that the point? After a time, still mesmerized by
the rabbits, I would put the paper and pencil down and sit,
absorbing the early evening air. Ruminating is easier than
writing. I caught myself worrying that I should be busier and
smiled at the irony. Slowly I began to shed the blanket, heavy
with the day's frenetic pace and distractions.

The cultural implication is that our identity is linked solely
to productivity, as if we are owned by the fear of dying without
accomplishing everything on our to-do list.

It's all about rewriting the codes. We've been wired this way
for so long, it's hard to stop. Just learning to say, "I'm doing
nothing," or "I'm watching rabbits," or "I'm big leaf dancing,"
without a grimace or need for further explanation takes
fortitude and resolve usually not found in our species. "The
problem is not simply that we work too much, the problem is
that we are working for the wrong reward. We are paid in the
wrong currency." Lynne Twist has it right:

> What if we were to expand our definition
> of wealth to include those things that grow

> only in time—time to walk in the park, time
> to take a nap, time to play with children,
> to read a good book, to dance, to put our
> hands in the garden, to cook playful meals
> with friends, to paint, to sing, to meditate,
> to keep a journal.

G. K. Chesterton once said that to go against the flow of cultural assumptions would be "like standing on our heads." Although there's no need to blame the culture, for more often than not, this flow makes up the white water cascading through our own minds. Either way, I say that it is time to give the judges and scorekeepers a day off.

Now that's living!

As I head off to weed the lower perennial bed behind our house, it hits me that the grass looks particularly inviting and soft—no doubt because it needed mowing. I tell myself that I will tackle it after the weeding, after which I'll work on the book, now close to its deadline—so why not boost my motivation with a brief power nap? I sprawl on the lawn and smell the sweetness of the earth; the sun's warmth is soothing on my face, a contrast to the cool of the grass on my back. I listen to the bees as they go about their day. I awake without awareness of time. A nap will do that for you, you know, give you an hour's break from needing to be productive or right all the time—an affliction leading to blindness to the natural world (not to mention your wife and children). I wake from my nap pleasantly disoriented and decide that the weeding can wait, as I just remembered a new rose that I needed to order and remembered again my need to work on the book. But I tell myself that, at the moment, I have no great insights, especially any that would warrant being tagged as helpful strategies for inner peace. Although I read about this man who heard that you gain inner peace when you finish everything you've already started. That sounded right, so he looked around and that afternoon finished off a bottle of red wine, his Prozac prescription, and a half a box of chocolates. "You have no idea how good I feel," he told anyone he saw.

I do know this, that I want to travel lighter, and it seems contradictory—by only exacerbating the problem—to add another to-do list to the menu necessary to make life worth living. After all, we can get oddly grandiose about this whole state of affairs. We can turn loving life into another contest. You know, if we're going to try this on for size, we might as well excel at it, as if we can become some sort of expert at loving life or productive stillness. You never know who might notice.

Have you heard the story about the wealthy Texan who designated in his will that he be buried in his Cadillac? True story. And his request was honored. At the burial, when the car was being rolled into the grave, a man was overheard saying, "Man, now that's living."

But it's more than that. It's the discomfiting implication that this day, as it currently stacks up, is not sufficient. It needs to be improved upon, made more respectable or enviable by some gadget or self-help course available on the shopping network for *only* three low monthly payments on our credit card.

I know this because I have invested my share of money in self-improvement schemes, which more often than not morph into a voracious black hole because—as it has been said—you can't get enough of what you don't really need.

Gladly, the full force of life usually envelops me when I'm looking the other way, say, for answers or magic or resolve. It is a lot like grace in that way. It enters in, slows the heartbeat, and before you know it, you're sitting still: relishing, contemplating, savoring, just being—if only for a moment. These moments re-introduce me to a world that is antithetical to the world that tells me the five things I must do to stay on top. Like yesterday, when on my way to the south end of the island, I saw a kingfisher, perched alert on the branch of a small tree overhanging an inlet of the sound. His sapphire coat looked lustrous against the pale blue sky, and he appeared, for all I could see, to be enjoying the afternoon sun, watchful in some pre-dinner-vigil-pose, and looking ever the fifties' tough guy, with his characteristic Brylecream-spiked crown. It is not often that you get to see a kingfisher, so I slowed to a crawl and felt the gooseflesh on my arms as I eased by, rubber-necking in my truck.

It happens when I'm sitting in my car on the ferry dock whiling away the time, waiting for the next ferry boat, and the late afternoon sun fills my car with some snooze-inducing narcotic, and the next thing I know I'm in and out of consciousness in a dreamy state, sensing that it doesn't get any better than this.

Or it happens on days like today, when it feels like the end of autumn. This is the weekend when the time changes or at least our perception of time changes. You can feel the weight of submission, the sense that something is slipping away, acquiescing. Daylight recedes as a murky dusk settles in by late afternoon, and darkness is with us long before supper is on the table. Even so, walking through the garden I am cheered by the final rose blooms that carry on, willful and determined, their allspice fragrance still heartwarming. I hear the muted echo of snare-drum brush strokes through the woods, as the leaves of the big leaf maples sprinkle and flutter and scatter, the days and nights now a theater in sense-around. In a week the trees will be completely bare, their winter skeletons becoming austere and resolute sentries against a sheet-metal-gray sky.

Into the fray of details

I know this for certain: People who love life embrace particularity. Particularity means not shying away from the details. In fact, particularity throws caution to the wind and jumps, whole hog, into the fray of details. It's about awareness. Noticing the specifics. It is the heart and core of all sacred necessities.

Particularity slows us down, stops us, and immerses us into the full weight, the density of the daily. See that bearded iris? That is not just a flower, it's smelling-salts for the soul. Above is not just an October sky, it's a viscous canopy, an unfolding drama alive with movement. I am a gardener because of particularity. I immerse myself in this liturgy of seasons, fueled with expectation and hope, nurture and commitment, protection and conserving, grieving and waiting, giving way each spring to expectation and hope once again. These are not lessons to be learned to prepare for life. This is my life. I also know that those of us who attempt to speak of such things lose something in the translation.

I told a friend the title of this book. She gave me a quizzical look, and then asked me, "So, do you love life?"

"Well," I told her, "not always. But I sure cherish the moments when I do."

This is a book about those moments. It is an invitation to pay attention.

But I must warn you. To pay attention, you must slow down.

I can give you the party line that slowing down is a tonic for the heart and pretty much a necessity for our blood pressure. It is restorative for our emotional well-being and nourishment for our soul. You pick the word: tonic, sustenance, nutriment, curative, balsamic, sanative. I have no doubt that they all ring true. People who know a lot more than I do tell me so. While we're sorting it out though, let's wander through the back garden and I'll tell you what I do know for certain.

I can tell you that there is a direct correlation between slowing down and joy. You know, that feeling which expands your chest and slows the world's carousel, so that everything and everyone around you is in crystal-clear focus, and your mind has no need for approval or scheming or regret. You are content merely to be. Just to be. As if the very emotion resides in that realm of time where the heartbeat slows.

I can tell you that when I slow down I pay attention, and I give up my need for control. I can tell you that Quaker theologian Thomas Kelly got it right when he wrote, "Listening to the eternal involves a silence within us." And I can tell you that when I slow down, I begin to live more openly and relaxed.

I can also tell you that it is a cool and blustery late October day, the kind of weather that sends up an unequivocal flare to let us know that summer has migrated south. Rain will be our companion for some time now. The shrubs and perennials do their best to stand tall against the southerly gusts. There are stubborn blooms on the antique roses *Souvenir de la Malmaison* and *Comte de Chambord*. They give the upper beds a certain dignity, an old world charm. Asters, verbena, and chrysanthemum all flower cheerfully though terribly sprawled, flopped, and askew. Nuthatches continue their resolute forays to the black-oiled sunflower-seed feeder, up and down the old fir tree as furtive and urgent bandits. Wispy clouds ride a river torrent through the sky, like a backdrop which has missed its cue and is hastily escorted across the stage. The air is touched with the smoke of wood stoves. And except for the nuthatches and an occasional stirring of the leaves, there is silence.

> **"If a country is governed wisely . . . people**
> **enjoy their food, take pleasure in being**
> **with their families, spend weekends**

working in their gardens, delight in the doings of the neighborhood."

—Tao Te Ching

"I may not have the answers, but I think

I'm asking the right questions."

—Rabbi Levine

Amazement

At the back of our brains, so to speak, there is a forgotten blaze or burst of astonishment at our own existence. The object of the artistic and spiritual life is to dig for this sunrise of wonder.

—G. K. Chesterton

1

Where I live, a June evening sky can be heart-rending. The sun oozes beyond the horizon, a melting shimmer over the Olympic Mountains. The clock, if one was available, would read past nine-thirty. The western sky remains backlit until well past ten. It is a blue light, giving the horizon a pulpy density, the clouds, trees, and mountains now notably substantive, more firmly anchored and more clearly burdened by gravity. The hues are now deeper, as if more expensive. Ralph Lauren couldn't have done better.

Stillness settles with the warm, dense summer air. At the moment of dusk, there is a noticeable pause, the earth catching its breath before beginning the cycle again.

I sit on the deck, in total amazement, applauding the dusk sky-pageant. My arms are chilled with gooseflesh.

This is not an easy task, merely to sit, with no chore but to absorb. To absorb only for the sake of absorbing, without appraisal, or brooding about whatever goads the mind from tomorrow's docket. It is a perpetual dilemma, that with my mind wired to tomorrow's promises, I run the risk of ruining the effect.

I am a novice to be sure, but sitting still is an art form I want to practice, learning to feel my heart beat slowly, celebrating the silhouettes of trees and mountains as they are imperceptibly swallowed by the inky curtain of the night.

Living in constant, total amazement

Joe Versus the Volcano is one of my favorite quirky movies. The title alone wins style points. Tom Hanks plays Joe, a young man stuck in his life, stuck in a job he detests, stuck in a windowless cubicle of florescent light. Is this all there is?

Joe spends his days seeking his doctor's advice for an endless litany of phantom illnesses. One day, a stranger introduces himself and offers Joe an opportunity, a way out.

Preying on Joe's fear of illness, the stranger tells him that he does indeed have a life threatening illness, a mysterious brain-cloud. The fact that this is a hoax, that such a malady does not exist, is beside the point. Joe resigns himself to his fate, that his days are numbered, which in turns gives him freedom to live his life. He welcomes the opportunity to carry out his new mission (offered by the stranger). Joe is to present himself to a small south sea island tribe where he is to be offered to appease the volcano god by jumping into an active, burning volcano.

Now that Joe realizes that life is short, time becomes precious. And as the movie goes on, Joe wakes up. At one point, watching the moon rise above the ocean horizon, Joe sums up his transformation: "Most people go through life asleep. But the ones who are awake live in constant total amazement."

One thing is certain. You cannot script amazement, awe, wonder, or delight. This is our visceral response to some gift of life. To Albert Einstein, our visceral response is the sign of life. "Whoever is devoid of the capacity to wonder, whoever remains unmoved, whoever cannot contemplate or know the deep shudder of the soul in enchantment, might just as well be dead, for he has already closed his eyes upon life."

Amazement.

It is a sacred necessity.

Children know this to be true. Amazement is standard fare in the life of a young child. Children live wide-eyed, giddy, curious, thrilled. We did. But then, somewhere along the way, we learned to trade amazement for acquiescence. Our sense of wonder was blunted, numbed, or rendered inactive.

Elizabeth Barrett Browning reminds us that "all of earth is aflame, but only those who see it take off their shoes," an allusion to the Old Testament story about Moses and the burning bush. I remember the story from Sunday school, Moses cowering near a ball of flame (in our books it looked like a tumbleweed on fire). Let's just say that it was not a story with much kid appeal compared, say, to Jonah and the whale. A guy who becomes fish bait beats a talking shrub every time.

But the shrub was on fire—divine spontaneous combustion of some sort—and to hear our teacher tell it, in a deep baritone voice (in the church of my youth, God always spoke in a male baritone voice) reads Moses his to-do list, beginning with, "Moses, take off your shoes. You're on holy ground." So Moses takes of his shoes. And it's no wonder. That baritone voice can scare the bejesus out of you. The preaching of my youth left its stain—something about being in the presence of a deity, shaking like a leaf. I always figured shoe removal was some kind of religious requirement.

Now, looking back, I believe I was wrong. It wasn't fear that Moses felt. It was amazement. I believe Moses removed his shoes to feel the soil, the sand, the earth. Remember when you were a kid? Remember those barefoot summer days—at the lake, the beach, or in the park—toes in the sand? Or hands in the mud? How your spine tingled and you couldn't believe your luck? Now that's holy ground.

I know a man who was given the task of childcare, watching two adolescent boys for an entire day. They were the children of a friend. Although childcare was neither his strong suit nor a special area of interest, he consented under duress. "The boys arrived at my house with their Game-Boy video games," he told me, "and it completely took me by surprise. I'm way out of touch. I guess I had completely panicked about what I needed to do to entertain them. But within minutes they were engrossed in their machines. Their faces were frozen, their bodies hunched over." Behind this man's house is a large hole, possibly left over from construction and never filled in. After an hour of watching them play, he asked if they would come outside to help him with a small project. He needed to move a few boards. "When the boys saw the hole, they raced into the bottom and asked if I had a hose," he said, laughing. They began to fill the hole with water. And they stayed there— in the mud—for the remainder of the day. Their Game-Boys remained on the deck, ignored, while they romped, smiled, laughed giddy with delight.

I can relate.

I moved to Vashon Island sixteen years ago because of my newfound love of gardening. I devoured every book that I could find about plants and about this new place I called home. Nurseries became my sanctuary. My heartbeat increased as I moved up and down the aisles, touching, smelling, and scrutinizing, beguiled by foliage and blooms. My hunger was voracious, so I started a journal just to see if I could figure out what had come over me. I filled it with observations and emotions, sketches and ideas, pictures and memories, plans and whims.

During that first spring in our new home, you could find me on my knees out in the back corner of the garden, hunched over in a comically bizarre pose, my face only a foot or so off the ground like some penitent religious zealot frozen in an exaggerated prayer. There I would be, painstakingly brushing the soil away, an archeologist, unearthing some heretofore-unseen treasure with exaggerated gentleness. I was looking for dahlia shoots. Dahlias are an autumn bloomer with large raucous-colored flowers, some reminding me of cheerleader pom-poms. My dahlias had not appeared yet, and I was duly worried that they were not alive, that something had happened while my guard was down. It is the gardener's neurosis: we're always certain that we've done something wrong. The books I consulted didn't seem to mollify me, in part because I am impatient and overanxious. And my equilibrium could not be copasetic until I knew the fate of my dahlias. After about an inch or so of excavation, I would find the object of my quest. There would be three or four pale shoots, wound tight and conical, still in hibernation, biding their time on their way up toward the sun. They were, apparently, not on my timetable. I would push the soil back, covering the shoots. I must confess there were some mornings I would wander back two or three times, digging around the same new shoots just to see what, if anything, had changed. As I dug, an almost conspiratorial tingling would shoot up through the base of my neck and into my brain. My arms were covered in gooseflesh. It was a heady mixture of intrigue and the excitable fervid energy that attends and veils any clandestine lover's rendezvous.

There are moments of amazement that seem just beyond the wherewithal of explanation. "I just don't have the words to describe it," I've heard people say, thunderstruck, and I know the feeling. In my rendezvous with my dahlias, these were emotions too good to be true, and I kept my ritual a secret. I was certain that to any outsider, my behavior looked silly, fodder for being played a fool.

I hadn't figured out what it all meant, this new infatuation with life, or how it would play itself out. But I did learn something fundamental: they are enough, these moments. That life, as Walt Whitman pointed out, "is contained in a moment." Marveling at the sight of those anemic buds is enough.

Now, in retrospect, I see that the stigma attached to such emotion is curious at best. At the time (for whatever reason),

I didn't want to own up to such intense feelings of joy. I am not altogether sure what I was afraid of, in the same way that I was not altogether sure what was transpiring in my own body (or soul for that matter). But I do know that this invigoration captured me wholly, and I became its wholehearted captive.

Do you recall a time when you knew that deep shudder of enchantment? Do you remember the last time you were in total amazement? "Yes," one man told the group at a recent seminar I was leading. "Watching my wife try to parallel park our car. I am completely amazed every time." There was a chorus of amens.

What we need is not a primer on "how to find amazement," but the permission to experience, to give in to, to give up control.

I have a friend, a Methodist minister, who found a love of gardening later in life. He told me about walking in a small public garden near his home. "I don't know what hit me," he said, "but I literally became unhinged." Edith Wharton calls it "garden magic . . . a sort of enchantment of place, an intoxication or spell that affects you in all the senses."

My friend's experience took him by surprise (as did my experience with the dahlias). "There was another time, " he told me. "I went back to the garden to walk and pray. But I was so enamored with it all, I couldn't focus on prayer. The fragrance of the lilies . . . I felt horribly guilty, until it hit me that this infatuation was my prayer." It reminded me of the "prayer" of the designer of New York's Central Park, Frederick Law Olmstead, while visiting Savannah, Georgia:

> On the other side, at fifty feet distant were
> rows of old live oak trees, their branches
> and twigs slightly hung with a delicate
> fringe of gray moss, and their dark, shining,
> green foliage meeting and intermingling
> naturally but densely overhead. The
> sunlight streamed through and played
> aslant the lustrous leaves and waving,
> fluttering, quivering, palpitating, pendulous
> moss: the arch was low and broad; the
> trunks were huge and gnarled; and there
> was a heavy groining of strong, dark, rough,
> knotty branches. I stopped my horse, bowed
> my head, and held my breath. I have never
> in all my life seen anything so impressively
> grand and beautiful.

A funny thing happened on the way to prayer. He found the sacred instead. There is something to be said for suspending control, especially our need for theological religious control. With theological control, we have predetermined God's place, God's reaction. We have left no room for surprise.

In the initial rush in my garden, there was no thought given to public opinion, and my energy burned myopic and consuming. Time stood still. Thankfully, analysis came much later, past the juncture when appraisal can throw a monkey wrench in the party.

But it wasn't just the joy. It was relishing being on the receiving end. I was at the mercy of something or someone outside of my control, bestowing blessings and goodness on my little corner of the world.

As time passed, there came a point when I felt the urge to pause and wonder: Why did all of this grab me so? As if there was a test due and some appropriate justification for this expenditure of joy would be required. As if joy had to be doled out in increments, metered, or hoarded like a savings account, never under any circumstances overdrawn. I would even go so far as to practice a defense in my mind, looking the imaginary jury in their eyes, just in case I was ever charged. Thankfully I never got very far, as I was always drawn back to the bud or flower, detoured by a butterfly, or captivated by the light and I would notice how if I stood just right, the sunlight would give our plum tree blossoms the look of an explosion with translucent confetti.

Spellbound by something we don't remember planting

To say that my new source of joy totally caught me by surprise sounds a bit disingenuous. The truth is, I had moved to this island because I wanted to get away from the hectic pace, the noise, and my distraction-prone lifestyle. I wanted to slow down. I didn't like who I was then, so captivated by the frenzy of exploit and reputation.

And yet, what is at stake here is not merely doing or acting (or even changing), but being acted upon or being done unto. Allowing one to be on the receiving end of some cosmic giveaway. Some heavenly sweepstakes (without the need to sit through the requisite ninety-minute presentation about time-share rentals).

There's a wonderful scene in the novel *Cold Mountain*, where Ada writes to her cousin:

> **Working in the fields, there are brief times when I go totally without thought. Not one idea crosses my mind, though my senses are alert to all around me. Should a crow fly over, I mark it in all its details, but I do not seek analogy for its blackness. I know it is a type of nothing, not metaphoric. A thing unto itself without comparison. I believe those moments to be the root of my new mien. You would not know it on me for I suspect it is somehow akin to contentment.**

It was the cultural mount-my-steed-and-slay-the-dragon mentality that I had to be weaned from. We're addictively fond of technology, and its marriage to our western ingenuity has birthed communication and technology miracles that boggle the mind. Starry-eyed by the magic of it all, we're prone to believe the hype on the label, and do our utmost to orchestrate some form of technology to solve any and every human conundrum. So we build and we fiddle, we race and we connive, and in the end, no further along, we give up tinkering, blessedly finding ourselves sitting on the ground in the garden in total amazement, spellbound by something we don't remember planting.

It's all about grace, isn't it? It doesn't take long to see that. Amazement is the emissary of grace, its container.

But however you slice it, grace is a tough sell in this culture. It doesn't package well for an infomercial. Which is, I suppose, precisely the point. Because there's no reason for this delivery, this package of grace. Moments without justification or merit are like stories without morals. They just flat-out go against our grain. You cannot balance the books here. You just have to sit and take it. And then let it wash over you, warm and serene and unmitigated.

When traveling, there is one constant for gardeners: opportunities to compare notes with others inflicted by the same fever. The range of conversation can be wonderfully elastic, covering plants and soil, weather and pests, garden design and the endless list of ongoing projects, including most of those still in the dream stage. Every gardener has pages and pages of projects in the dream stage, and when they talk about them, their voices expand with the air of Christmas morning.

During one of my visits to Monument, Colorado, in the middle of a spread of bedroom communities between Denver and Colorado Springs, I spent some time touring the garden of Mrs. Eileen Sanderson. Mrs. Sanderson, in her seventies, has lived in this particular house for nearly twenty-six years, and was in no hurry to move anyplace else. A friend of mine suggested to Mrs. Sanderson that I drop by for a garden visit.

Bird feeders, easily fifteen to twenty, were stationed here and there around the property near the house. Some were filled with her special recipe of melted peanut butter and suet. We talked about the feathered visitors we both had been lucky to receive during the past year and the similarities and differences between Colorado and western Washington.

In the front of her home stood a juniper shrub, easily seven feet in height and about three or so feet in width, in effect blocking the window, which looks out from the kitchen breakfast nook. The shrub is odd looking, and by all accounts should be removed or at least dramatically pruned. There is an exterior ledge from the breakfast nook window that appears to link with the hedge. Birds feed in the juniper as well as on the window ledge. "Once I crack open that window," Mrs. Sanderson tells me as if reading my mind while I stared at the hedge, "my birds seem to know. They descend from everywhere into that shrub for their snack. It wouldn't be a good day if we couldn't spend some time with our birds."

We were standing in her front garden area, a few feet or so from the front entry flanked by this Ritz-Carlton for birds juniper. She laughed. "I know that landscapers wouldn't approve of this shrub. It blocks the window and makes for a kind of dark entrance. But then I don't really care what the landscapers think." She paused and added, "I certainly could never bring myself to take it down. These birds bring me so much joy."

It was the way she said it that got me. There was nothing feigned or artificial in her voice. It was pure, unalloyed joy. I realize that I am one of the lucky ones. Her joy rubbed off on me that day, and has stayed with me ever since.

Where do you have to go to be amazed?

This is our ingrained response: Where do we get what she had? Let's find the product called amazement, bottle it, sell it, and retire to the Caribbean.

But the question is not completely unrealistic. Is amazement a learned skill? Do we go to gooseflesh seminars? Or buy a book called *Enchantment for Dummies*? I saw a magazine touting an article "10 Places to Be Overwhelmed." I had to scratch my head and chuckle. Why is it that we need to go somewhere else to experience life in its fullness?

Isn't that the conundrum? The voice that tells us we must add something else to our lives; something else that is, apparently, not there. And in the end, we miss the point. Whatever it is has been there the entire time we were so fervently searching.

It may be a scene, a relationship, or an inconvenience, something looked at daily, but never really seen. There's a wonderful instance of this in Yann Martel's great novel, *Life of Pi*:

> **I described Mr. Kumar's place as a hovel. Yet
> no mosque, church, or temple ever felt so
> sacred to me. I sometimes came out of that
> bakery feeling heavy with glory. I would
> climb onto my bicycle and pedal that glory**

through the air. One such time I left town and on my way back, at a point where the land was high and I could see the sea to my left and down the road a long ways, I suddenly felt I was in heaven. The spot was in fact no different from when I had passed it not long before, but my way of seeing it had changed. That feeling, a paradoxical mix of pulsing energy and profound peace, was intense and blissful.

Amazement takes root in the simple sentence, "I never noticed that before." I am welcoming life, inviting it in, not allowing internal censors and judges to scrutinize the making certain that this moment passes muster. In moments of amazement, we render our internal scorekeeper mute. There is a good deal of conjecture about who merits this streak of luck and why. Some people get all the moments of astonishment. Or, perhaps, they've allowed themselves to see. Either way, these moments sustain us. Create a fabric in our soul which absorbs daily miracles.

Amazement has become an atrophied muscle. When it is out of use, it remains dormant. Perhaps it can be jump-started with a few questions: Do you realize what you just saw? Witnessed? Experienced?

I believe that amazement is an antidote to apathy.

Why does it fuel me? Why does it give me reason to go on? Is there a world without wonder?

In the mountains above Antigua, Guatemala, I visited a family in their new home, which had been built by Habitat for Humanity. This house was special because it was the fifteen-thousandth house built in Guatemala. My friend worked for Habitat and had a special relationship with this particular family. He wanted to help them with a housewarming gift. My friend bought six fruit trees and two bougainvillea vines. I tagged along as the garden expert, to help plant and provide care instructions.

The lot was small, bare ground save for a few weeds, the soil a reddish silt. In the middle of the lot sat the new house, a square concrete block building with a metal roof. It measured 500 square feet and consisted of four rooms. The family—father, mother, and two children—was thrilled.

I spent an hour or so digging holes in which to place the trees. La Señora stood at the doorway, her face in a fixed smile, perhaps fearing that if she moved her good fortune would disappear. I stopped to wipe the sweat from my brow and to take a swig from the can of cola they had offered me. In the digging . . . there is no hierarchy. We are both participants in this sunrise of wonder.

Amazement and particularity

We're back to that part about particularity. You know, attention to detail. Seek wonder, go smaller. The majesty is in the diminutive, the details. Have you ever seen a passionflower blossom? It is a finely layered cake in three-dimensional relief. It is a miniature handcrafted native American headdress created for a festival to fertility. It is a world unto itself. "I discovered that my own little postage stamp of native soil was worth writing about, and that I would never live long enough to exhaust it," William Faulkner said. Enamored by that which is huge and grandiose, we eventually give way to boredom and apathy. Drawn to the particular, to the details, we are taken through the wardrobe to Narnia.

November weather does not arrive in the Northwest. It sweeps in, like some cantankerous and peevish diva. She assaults the air, stirring with incessant and capricious waves of her hands. With each wave of low pressure comes a storm, followed by a moment of calm. Wind and rain, followed by sun breaks, followed by wind and rain. If we are unlucky, which happens more often than not, the cloud settles in for a few days, and rain seeps unrelenting like a leaky ceiling painted a morose gray. Everyone I know hates November because it is a worse than lousy month of weather. But even so, it's still the best time to see an extraordinary rainbow.

From our house, we see rainbows out over the Puget Sound, appearing to dissolve into the water, or stretch into the mountains hinting at those childhood lands of make-believe. Sometimes they seem to stretch across the entire Seattle basin, as if linking the Cascade Mountains to the Olympics. Sometimes they appear so frequently we don't bother to stop and look. But this past November, my wife and I witnessed a miracle, the kind of phenomenon that makes you feel like one of those shepherds gazing at the great star over Bethlehem. A rainbow literally ended in our canyon, not more than a hundred yards or so from our deck. I've never seen a rainbow end. Well, end or begin, we couldn't tell. But there it lingered. It had the consistency of a well-defined apparition, each color band lucid, even though the misting rain gave it the appearance of metallic sprinkles. It was as if it was being poured from a heavenly spout, the way it arched perfectly to the ground, or as if it was a spotlight, illuminating some secret spot—not unlike the beacons you see in movies about alien spacecraft, with great shafts of light shot from their underbellies to the ground, used as transportation, beaming unwitting earthlings aboard the visiting ship.

If you never have seen something before, analysis doesn't seem to do the trick. Only sitting still will do. There is an instinctive wash of wonderment, as if all of the pores open to be more receptive, as if your body knows better than you do, that this is holy ground and whatever else you were doing can wait.

Sanctuary

It's not the number of breaths you take
that gives you life, but how many moments
take your breath away.

—Anonymous

2

ach afternoon, the son of a famous rabbi would return home from school, put his backpack on the dining table, and leave the house through the kitchen door. The young boy would run into a wooded area not far away. He spent thirty minutes—give or take—every school day afternoon in the woodland. His father knew of his son's peculiar habit but said nothing. After a matter of weeks, however, the rabbi grew concerned. "Is my son up to mischief?" he wondered. So he decided to broach the subject.

"Tell me, son," he asked one afternoon after his son returned from his woodland visit. "Why do you spend each afternoon in the woodland? What are you doing out there?"

"Papa," the boy replied, "don't worry. I go to the woodland every day. It is my special space, because there I can talk with God."

"Oh," the father said, visibly relieved. "I am glad to hear it. But you, the son of a rabbi, should know that God is the same everywhere."

"Yes, Papa. I know that God is the same everywhere. But I am not."

The rabbi's son knew something about spaces. We all have two spaces in our lives. In the one there is activity, productivity, accomplishment, achievement, busyness, and a fair bit of stress. In this space we have our calendars, our pagers, our cell phones, our palm pilots and our to-do lists. In this space we work, we achieve, and we produce.

But there is another space. This is the space for stopping, for reflection, contemplation, and meditation. In this space is born prayer, music, poetry, friendship, amazement, awe, wonder, and if we are fortunate, unrepentant napping.

This is the sacred necessity of sanctuary, sanctuary as sacred space.

Sanctuaries do not just happen

Sanctuaries are created with intention. They do not just happen. If we do not see the distinction, perhaps it is because we already have sanctuaries, sacred spaces in our lives, but do not recognize them.

St. Andrew's Abbey is a ninety-minute drive from civilization. Civilization is that code word for any place people scurry about and drive hell-bent for leather. I wind through the hills on the north side of the San Gabriel Mountains, above Pasadena, California. When I turn my rental car into the driveway I instinctively slow down. After a quarter of a mile or so, I enter the grounds passing a familiar sign (showing its age, now leaning against a tree), "No Hunting Except For Peace." I take my cell phone from its holster and turn it off. Not that it matters, as there is no reception in these mountain foothills.

I am beginning a one-week retreat. Predictably, I rushed to arrive on time, so I am early, which means that my room is not yet ready. As a Benedictine monastery, St. Andrew's is well known for its hospitality. Anyone is welcomed as a retreatant. I walk to the eucalyptus grove beyond the guest rooms. There are perhaps sixty to eighty trees, a few older than me. My guess is sixty years old or more. It is one of the few places in the area where grass grows, protected from the unrelenting high desert sun.

As I enter this glen under an olive tree, there is a perceptible drop in temperature. It is as if one has truly entered a sanctuary, a room designed for sitting a spell. Like the old man in his rocking chair, asked by some passerby, "So old man, whatcha' doing?" He rocked and smoked his pipe and replied, "How soon you need to know?"

I sit in a plastic lawn chair and remind myself, "I'm here to work." After all, I've come to write. There is much to do and only a week to accomplish it.

My body is still racing. So I stop, doing my best to pay attention. I recognize the residual effect of my requisite Starbucks double latte consumed earlier that morning. I'm acclimated to a certain pace, as if there's some internal governor with the pedal to the metal, and downshifting is tough to do. I admit to myself, begrudgingly, that I'm here not just to write. I'm here to downshift. And I know that this is one of my sanctuaries, sacred spaces, precisely because it allows me to shift gears. Not that downshifting is all that easy. I'm humored by the thought, "I wish I had time just to sit and do nothing." As if. Well, here I am. With time to do nothing. And my mind is jittery, already needing a distraction.

Behind me grows a honeysuckle vine, covering a pergola. A hummingbird hovers, no doubt piqued by my intrusion on his turf. I remember the first time my spiritual director told me to spend time in this grove. It was almost twenty years ago. He gave me a pad of paper and pencil, and asked me to spend twenty or thirty minutes alone, silent, listening, in order to "write down whatever God tells you."

Right. Clearly I had not heard him correctly.

"Let me get this straight," I ask for clarification. "You want me to take this paper and pencil and to sit near the trees and write down whatever God tells me?"

He nods. He's either not right in the head or I have entered the twilight zone.

"Okay," I tell him gamely.

When I returned after my requisite thirty minutes, I confessed my inability. "Apparently I didn't understand the assignment."

"But your notebook is full," he notices.

"Of course it's full, I had thirty minutes to kill out there. I needed something to do to keep from going stir crazy."

He reads my list aloud. "Change oil in car." He laughs.

"Hey," I protest. "It's my to-do list for the week. Not all of us can spend our days sitting among the trees listening to God."

"Okay," he tells me, "but who are you to tell God that he can't be involved in your oil change?"

He laughs.

I get the point.

A sanctuary helps us to stop and pay attention

Sanctuaries are those sacred spaces, those places, where we stop and pay attention. They provide a way of sanctifying time. They release time from the demand that it measure up or produce, from the requisite questions:

"Did you use your time wisely?"

"Why are you wasting so much time?"

"That wasn't a very good use of time, was it?"

Sanctuaries are those spaces, those places, in which, as Maya Angelou observed, "no problems are confronted, no solutions searched for. Each of us needs to withdraw from the cares which will not withdraw from us." In this space the focus is replenishment.

It is well known that Ghandi spent a good deal of time at his spinning wheel. Yes, he enjoyed spinning, but it was more than that. He talked about his wheel as the place (the space) where he could remove himself from the pressing demands and issues of the day. A place where he could be centered, calm, rejuvenated. It was his sanctuary. His sacred space.

Do we make this sacred space? We can. I have one friend who created a prayer garden. It's a patio made of stone, with a bench surrounded by lavender and rosemary. The garden is tucked away from the main garden, hidden by shrubbery. It's her own secret garden, her sanctuary.

I have another friend who has a solitude seat. She put an old Adirondack chair in the woods behind her house. It's in a little clearing under an old cedar tree. "I go there when I don't want anyone to bother me," she says in a tone that tells me she means it. In his book *The Wildest Place on Earth*, John Mitchell talks about the garden as such a place, "something you can get a sense of, a center, an intimate, organized space where you can go to get away from the world—not something that a passerby on the road can see and then comment upon."

At a recent seminar, one couple listened to my talk about Sabbath and sanctuary, and the husband told me their story. "Last year we finished building a new home. It was going to be our dream house. So we spent a lot of time and energy working on the design. But after I saw the plans I knew something wasn't right, even though it eluded me. And then it hit me. Where am I going to sit with my cup of coffee and read the paper every morning? After hearing your talk, I realized that this morning ritual is my sacred space, it is important to my sanity and my well being, and I needed my architect to consider that in the house design." The result was a nook off the kitchen that looked out over a ravine near their home.

We can find sanctuary created by an intentional morning ritual. At age ninety-three, the great cellist Pablo Casals said that "for the past eighty years I have started each day in the same manner. . . . I go to the piano, and I play two preludes and fugues of Bach. . . . It is sort of a benediction on the house. But that is not its only meaning. . . . It is a rediscovery of the world in which I have the joy of being a part. It fills me with awareness of the wonder of life, with a feeling of the incredible marvel of being human."

The garden. The woodland. A house nook. At the piano. Or, on a football field. I heard Bill Parcels, a highly respected coach in the NFL, talk about football practice that way. "It is my sanctuary. I feel cloistered there."

It is obvious that there are no hard and fast rules. Sometimes we create that space within the frenzied time and space of a workday, as if we are inside a bubble. A child of early television, I have the image of the cone of silence, the plastic bubble descending over Maxwell Smart and Chief on the *Get Smart* series. Sitting on a crowded subway, we close our eyes, take a deep breath, let it out slowly, and we are transported. This moment is not about time any longer. It is about refueling, reconnecting. It is sanctuary.

Creating sacred space is often a deliberate act, as Marcia Falk expresses in her poem, "Will."

> **Three generations back
> my family had only**
>
> **to light a candle
> and the world parted.**
>
> **Today, Friday afternoon,
> I disconnect clocks and phones.**
>
> **When night fills my house
> with passages,**
>
> **I begin saving
> my life.**

A slight breeze moves through the eucalyptus glen. In the air is a sweet, clean fragrance that I can't quite name. The sky is completely open, a robin's egg blue. I reach for my cell phone. It is not there. This is not easy work.

In a sanctuary we change our focus

In all of the instances above, there is one common denominator. Sanctuary, sacred space, allows us to pay attention. We change focus. My life is spent juggling—time, responsibilities, obligations, commitments, business, family, emergencies. It's easy to assume that the answer is better organization. All I need is a more sophisticated BlackBerry, a book on more creative goal-setting, or a CD with motivational music. It goes against the grain of our culture to say that the answer to our busyness is to stop, tend to the other space, find a sanctuary. A Sabbath. This is not just a day off. It is what Wayne Muller calls: "the presence of something that arises when we consecrate a period of time to listen to what is most deeply beautiful, nourishing, or true. It is time consecrated with our attention, our mindfulness, honoring those quiet forces of grace or spirit that sustain and heal us."

In a way, my blinders come off, if only for a short time.

In these sanctuary spaces, these Sabbath spaces . . . I'm giving up the need to arrive at some destination . . . I'm giving up my need for accomplishment.

It's not about what I get done or how I perform. My focus has changed. If I'm lucky, I take this new focus back into the other space. Dag Hammarskjold wrote, "The more faithfully you listen to the voice within you, the better you will hear what is sounding outside. And only he who listens can speak."

Sanctuary can be found even in the most profane of places

I am sitting with a group of twenty. We form a circle in the center of a campus meeting room. It is the first day of a training weekend, sponsored by a large urban university. The walls on two sides of the room are glass. We can watch the world go about its business. On one side is a patio with tables and chairs. On the other side, a construction site, teeming with activity, like a drama played out, the foreman shouting roles, directing the scene. It could be a new building, or it could be a parking lot, it's hard to tell. But the bustle and ado, with great earthmovers belching exhaust, seem a sure sign of renovation and progress.

Although it is early morning, voices surge in the air, barking above the rumble of the machines. Enormous excavators make short work, filling dump trucks using buckets that look like the jaws of a Tyrannosaurus. The incessant piercing signals of machines in reverse—like gunshots fired—rankle the nerves. Men in yellow safety helmets traverse the site. From inside the glass walls, it is as if we are watching the ritual of some leviathan ant farm. Some of the workers walk alone. Others stand in clumps of two or three. A few point and gesture. There are those who look as if they are on a mission. Others as if they are pacing, confused or lost, walking back and forth, marking time.

Twenty feet from our windows is the eight-foot high chainlink security fence that separates us from the work site.

Inside our room, we are in the middle of a morning prayer liturgy. Someone has just read from the book of Isaiah, "Let the wilderness and the thirsty land be glad, let the desert rejoice and burst into flower."

Inside our room, we hear the sound of trickling water, a small fountain that spills over stone. Above that are strains of soothing music. An oasis has been created. The floor is set up as a meandering stream bed made of richly colored sheets of cloth, surrounded by random stones, and small clay pots filled with ferns. Even so, we are not spared from the noise, disruption, and aggravation of the scene that borders us.

Our leader reads, "Let the desert rejoice and burst into flower." And then he asks us to consider the question, "What have been the sources of greening power in your life, those sources that allow you to rejoice and those areas of your life which burst into flower?" In the background we hear the incessant puncturing sound of construction machines.

My mind wanders. What I'm thinking is that I prefer to pray at a lakefront, on vacation, with the sun shining, with my bills paid (confident that my car doesn't need an oil change), knowing that my family loves me, and having just come from my therapist who has reminded me that in spite of all evidence to the contrary, I'm okay. I prefer to pray where the air is still, and across the lake I hear the echoes of the supplicating cry of a loon.

My reverie is interrupted by another bleating truck. Our leader says, "Let us pray."

It is Friday, my departure day from the monastery. I can feel the difference in my body. My heartbeat has increased, or at least has turned up the volume. I feel my nerves, the adrenaline, a sense of focus bracing itself, steeling itself for life on the outside of this space. Adrenaline preparing itself for a world of multitasking, noise, speed, bombardment of the senses, and deadlines. As I stop at the intersection before I steer my rental car onto the road outside the monastery, I pause, for only a moment, reminding myself that I take the gentle spirit of sanctuary with me.

"Listening to the eternal involves a

silence within us."

—Thomas Kelly

"There is a light lifting of the air so I can

smell the earth for the first time, and yesterday

I again took possession of my life here."

—May Sarton

Stillness

"This is one of our fears of quiet; if we stop and listen, we will hear this emptiness. . . . But this emptiness has nothing at all to do with our value or our worth. All life has emptiness at its core; it is the quiet hollow reed through which the wind of God blows and makes the music that is our life. Without that emptiness, we are clogged and unable to give birth to music, love, and kindness."

—Wayne Muller

3

Thundershowers just bullied their way through the area, dumping a good half inch or so of rain in an hour, and scaring the dickens out of my dogs. They don't get along with thunder. It has to be pretty deafening to rouse Penny (our oldest golden retriever). She doesn't hear well, as she is almost completely deaf. But maybe that's not so bad. (It reminds me of a line from a Jimmy Buffett song about his dad, "He was losing his hearing, but that's okay, because he doesn't care what most people say.")

The storm leaves the sky that shade of hunker-down gray, as if the ceiling tarp has been cinched at the corners, and some of the air gets let out through the cracks at the ends. It isn't so bad unless you had other things in mind for the weekend, like outdoor work. But what can you do? So you pop on a CD of Beethoven sonatas, curl up on the couch, catch up on magazine reading, and write a letter to a friend, who, if the mood strikes him, might even return the favor.

In the end it all turns out okay, until it comes time for the internal auditor to balance the books, and you have to justify whatever in the world you were doing all afternoon. Only then do you discover that apparently "hunkering down" isn't on the approved list.

And the war wages on—between that part of me which sets goals and sees accomplishment as valid and essential, and that part of me which relishes the hour when the silt-of-the-afternoon and blessed nothing washes over me. It's all about letting both selves, both slices of me, vie for space. Treating this dispute as a battle where there must be winners and losers means obliging a war—the battle we referred to in chapter two—with no end in sight. This seems obvious. Or so one would think.

Meanwhile, the rain has quit, it's time to get off the couch and head outside. I have some digging to do.

What would you like to be when you grow up?

The seeds of this war were planted long ago.

"What are you going to be when you grow up?" The question begins somewhere around age three and doesn't stop until the eulogizers wax eloquent with reverie. Apparently, there is no age that exempts you from being tested.

Our litany of responses ran the gamut, depending upon the year in school, the particular fad or interest, and the pressure from our parents and teachers. "Policeman, fireman, doctor, farmer, lawyer, or chief." Or, at about age nine, my own audacious, "I'm going to be the president of the United States." Hey, why not? It always got me a pat on the head. Not that I ever really wanted to be president. But it was the John F. Kennedy era, and my mother thought it was a good idea. In any event, I entered a contest (writing a letter to our state senator about the dream to become president) and won a full set of encyclopedias. I got my picture in the local newspaper, which is pretty impressive to a nine-year-old, and netted several more pats on the head.

Although in retrospect, we have not yet answered the question (the one older folk keep asking us about our vocations) have we? I mean, I was certain that I was going to "be somebody." Which in translation meant that I was going to accomplish something by having a vocation of value. But there's the point. I was going to do, and not be. My significance would be tied to my nametag and my paycheck. So I knew *what* I wanted to be, I just didn't know *whom.*

I love May Sarton's answer to the question, "What would you like to be?" As in, "what would you like to be when you grow up?" As in, "what should we chisel on your tombstone?"

"Human," she would reply simply. "I hope that I will be human."

I think that she was right. Exactly right. Now that is a journey worth taking.

We're all familiar with the tug of war between being and doing. Alan Lightman writes about his summers on a small island in Maine, a place where there are no cars, no telephones, no fax machines, no e-mail. He writes about his friend who motors over from the mainland for dinners and visits.

> George doesn't go anywhere without his cellular phone, even when having a leisurely dinner with me on the island. He claims to need it for incoming business calls, but I've never seen him receive any. I

believe the phone is a dutiful connection to
some other life, which he must constantly
rub against whether he wants to or not, just
as I find myself unable to stop visualizing
the other, time-ridden world or measuring
the duration of sunsets. We joke about it but
cannot change our behavior, cannot fully
capture our freedom.

This is the chain that gets yanked every time, as I am still
hoping that my worth is wedded to my busyness and my
DayTimer. If you take away that safety net, what are you
left with? What if grace didn't give a tinker's dam about my
busyness? What if I am accepted, just for being?

"Millions long for immortality who do not
know what to do with themselves on a rainy
Sunday afternoon."

—Susan Ertz

To be or to do, that is the question

An American traveler planned a long safari to Africa. He
was a compulsive man, loaded down with maps, timetables,
and agendas. Coolies had been engaged from a local tribe to
carry the cumbersome load of supplies, luggage, and "essential
stuff."

On the first morning, they all awoke very early and traveled
very fast and went very far. On the second morning, they all
awoke very early and traveled very fast and went very far. On

the third morning, they all awoke very early and traveled very fast and went very far. And the American seemed pleased. On the fourth morning, the jungle tribesmen refused to move. They simply sat by a tree. The American became incensed. "This is a waste of valuable time. Can someone tell me what is going on here?"

The translator answered, "They are waiting for their souls to catch up with their bodies."

Yes.

I wanted my soul back.

It was as simple as that. I just didn't figure it involved sitting still.

Whatever is human in us gets lost or devoured in our manic pace. And to regain it, we need to practice the scared necessity of stillness. The pleasure of slowness.

Thomas Merton, the well known Trappist monk and activist, tells about a revelation he had while sitting alone in the woods with his Coleman lantern. He is confronted with the fate that Coleman has constructed its lantern with a pragmatic intention over and above the simple provision of light. The packing box declares that the lantern "stretches days to give more hours of fun." Merton asks rhetorically, "Can't I just be in the woods without any special reason?"

He goes on to say that, in fact,

> **We are not having fun, we are not 'having' anything, we are not 'stretching our days,' and if we had fun it would not be measured by hours. Though as a matter of fact that**

> **is what fun seems to be: a state of diffuse
> excitation that can be measured by the
> clock and 'stretched by an appliance.'**

Perhaps Merton is onto something here. The possibilities are truly limitless: Fun-inducing appliances, coupled with an industry that helps us justify our time. Our closets are filled with gadgets designed to do just that. Don't tell the computer trade that you heard it here first.

What is it about our insidious need to assign value to every act or expenditure of time? As in, "Did you get anything done this morning?" Or, upon returning from any vacation for R & R, we are quizzed, "Well, what did you do?" We lump anything not of value into that great compost bin contrived to amass our wasted time.

A nap is approved if I've worked hard enough to deserve it, or if I'm feeling under the weather. A day off is condoned if it is my due. A loll through the garden is acceptable only if I pull some weeds on the way through. A wasted afternoon is allowed so long as it doesn't happen too often, and I seem duly contrite.

But it's deeper that all of that, isn't it? It seems that our perception of what is real is distorted. Real becomes anything of use, in other words, anything that has market value or is of pragmatic significance. The afternoon then, can no longer be just celebrated. It has to be used judiciously. Which takes some mental gymnastics when that use is soaking in a hot tub, reading a mystery, or watching your six-month-old son gurgle and slap at a mobile, or admiring the hummingbirds as they wage turf wars near the feeders off the back deck.

The fear of wasted time is a tough demon to exorcise. This makes stillness the sacred necessity with a price tag. But once you've wasted an afternoon in the garden—have tasted stillness—you get the sense that the medicine is itself blessedly fatal, so instead of fighting it with some stern and dour sounding work-ethic-inner-voice, you might just as well plop down on a garden bench and squander a few minutes (or even a day), and give this slowing-down-vaccine a whirl.

Come into the garden with me and let stillness cast its spell on you. It begins to work its power as the fragrance of the Asiatic lily 'casablanca' rolls over you in waves. It is a surprise attack, for it takes you a minute to locate the source, as the plant stands some thirty feet from the deck where you are reclining. So you smile and lean your head back as a red-tail hawk navigates the unseen currents high above. He seems content just to float, and his flight works as a sedative which calls for a short afternoon nap. The warmth of the afternoon sun settles around you and a duo of hummingbirds provides a grand theater with the cajoling and obdurate chatter that accompanies their ongoing turf war. Just before you drift off, you hear the bees' determined buzzing as they squeeze their chubby bodies in and out of the tubular flowers of the penstemon that sags and slouches near the garden bench.

As Kurt Vonnegut's uncle taught him to say, "If this isn't nice, what is?"

You gotta' admit, there's an allure to keeping busy

One editor told me that this scene was not believable. Real people don't have the time to just linger in their gardens. Real people are up to their gills in real time with real consuming dilemmas and real pressing duties.

"You must be talking about my newborn son," I told the editor. "He decides that if he can't sleep, no one else should have the luxury."

The editor looked at me as if I needed medical attention.

Did you know that the Chinese pictograph for the word busy is a combination of two other words? The words are: heart and kill. This little piece of language trivia will make you sit up and take notice. Here's a culture, several thousand years older than our own, which knows that activism and overwork are, borrowing from Thomas Merton again, "a pervasive form of contemporary violence." Merton goes on to say:

> . . . the rush and pressure of modern life
> are a form, perhaps the most common
> form, of innate violence. To allow oneself
> to be carried away by a multitude of
> conflicting concerns, to surrender to too
> many demands, to commit oneself to too
> many projects, to want to help everyone in
> everything, is to succumb to violence. The
> frenzy of our activism neutralizes our work
> for peace. It destroys our own inner capacity
> for peace. It destroys the fruitfulness of our

**own work, because it kills the root of inner
wisdom which makes work fruitful.**

My father is a brick mason. I'm biased, but he is without
argument, a fine craftsman, his work among the best I've ever
seen. He works with his hands. He works in the weather. And
he works by the sweat of his brow. From the time he was a
teenager until now, in his seventies, with no quit in sight. And
his word was, and is, his bond. If he told you he would do
something, it was a promise, and you could bet your paycheck
on it.

I learned the value of labor from my father. Well,
begrudgingly learned. At thirteen I was old enough to be
a hod-carrier (mixing mortar with a long handled hoe and
hauling cement blocks and bricks) during my summers while
my friends played. The labor was real, end-of-the-day-muscle-
ache real. I envied my friends.

I knew early on that my dad had no use for lazy workers. Or
lazy people for that matter. "Don't you have something you
could be doing?" he'd ask whenever I would be standing by
watching him work. He also couldn't understand how some
folk could look you in the eye, telling you they'd do one thing,
and do another. I still remember his asides about anyone with
no apparent drive or effort. And even more so, his ire for those
who simply chose not to work at all. "Who do you think foots
the bill for those bastards? Government handouts . . ." his line
of thought always trailing off in exasperation, outbursts surely
meant to be rhetorical.

But the sentiment went beyond just work. The implication was clear: It is a necessity to stay busy. Like most of my generation, I was weaned on the maxim that idle hands are the devil's tools. Even though I was not completely clear about its implications, it inferred the devil and that was enough to frighten me. I was brought up in a world where wasting time was a mortal sin, in a world where telling someone you were doing nothing was tantamount to confessing a Charles Mansonesque atrocity. These are schooling themes not easily weeded out when adulthood rolls around and life's lessons are ours for the making. This is the sort of stuff that saturates the pores.

And it is, by all accounts, venomous.

We could get a second opinion, but what's the use? So, the way I figure it, let's go ahead and face up to our time-honored predilections, admitting that we are indeed enamored by, fueled by, devoted to, and consigned to busyness. It feeds something deep down, its appetite voracious. And it feels . . . well I've got to tell you, sometimes it feels oh-so-good.

"Have you been staying busy?" friends will ask.

"Keeping busy, I hope," co-workers will remark.

"Staying busy, I see," an acquaintance will observe.

They are simple footnotes, really. And if I know the way the diversion works, I will respond without hesitation, "Busy? But of course. What, are you kidding, I've never been busier!"

I am taking a break from writing this morning, reading snippets from a recent *New Yorker* magazine. The back cover is an advertisement for a four-wheel-drive vehicle. Leaning against the driver-side mirror is the vehicle's owner (I assume), and placed elegantly around the owner are various items which (we are led to believe) were taken out of the vehicle. (It helps the effectiveness of the advertisement if we are really impressed.) The ad reads, "THE DREADED TO-DO LIST." And it lists: *"Samples to convention / Pick of Erika's skis / Work out / Pick up chair / Tee Time . . . 7 am / Salmon for BBQ / Lumberyard—Deck supplies / Nursery—shrubs / Go over contracts / Family weekend getaway—Toronto?"* Three or four of the items have been crossed off with pencil.

The bullying reality of the to-do list I can relate to. God knows I've got my own chronic list—transferred two or three times from paper scrap to paper scrap—awaiting me after my morning of writing.

But the magazine ad is certainly more than that.

What is it I am being sold here? A car?

Right.

A way of life perhaps? "Just think, dear reader, with a handful of cash (well, maybe two or three handfuls), you can accomplish much, not to mention that you can be terribly successful and wonderfully efficient."

Well, hey. I admit it. I envy this guy. After all, isn't that what they want? To get us to swallow this presumption that we can marry pell-mell and leisure with the right vehicle? Or maybe it's the presumption that we can marry pell-mell and leisure at all.

And deep down I'm thinking, "We still don't get it, do we? What kind of way is this to live? Must we remain perpetual slaves to this lurking requirement that we must have it all and do it all?" Difficult questions to entertain while the other side of me daydreams about cars and bank accounts which will resolve personal dilemmas and give meaning to my days.

We have things to do. Them's just the facts. More often than not, very pressing things. I felt the urgency earlier today when my neighbor called. There are only two houses along our canyon road, over a mile of undulating gravel. With our weather, it needs nursing every couple of years. It's time again, and my neighbor had a bit of time this morning to talk about fixing up the road. I hate being interrupted. Especially this morning, when I'm getting things done.

"Okay," I consented. "I'll meet you at the bottom of the hill."

The walk from my house down to our studio in the canyon is a quarter mile dirt-driveway hike through a canopy of massive big leaf maple trees and skyscrapers of hemlock and fir. I was jogging down, to get this over with. Ahead of me, on the driveway, in a spot where the foliage ceiling had split, shafts of sunlight danced and cavorted.

As if emerging from a mine, I froze and stared for awhile, a lone spectator to this late morning light caper and drama. After a few minutes, I walked slowly toward this stage of light.

High above me, elaborate dew misted spider webs were illumined, glistening jewels previously cloaked by the murky ceiling of the woods. It all caught me off guard. And I felt lucky, and, for the briefest of moments, forgot why I was in such a hurry.

We fill our days indefinitely preparing to live

The demon is our insistence that time is meant to be filled. If it is not consumed, it must be thrown away—like food which spoils—and deemed useless. What's more, wasting time carries a moral price tag with a requisite of guilt, implying that we will look back on our days through bifocals of regret.

Thankfully, there's a cleaning service in my town which advertises that they will "put the leisure time back into your life." Now there's customer service with a capital C. And even though we smile that cynical smile, it still gnaws at us, wondering if maybe there's something to this, and why not give it a whirl for a month or two. I mean, what's a few more dollars when sanity is at stake.

Trouble is, there's an implicit indictment to fessing up. You know, admitting we don't quite have a handle on our time, living betwixt and between and all that—that tug of war between obligations and personal sanity. Such a confession is not very impressive for someone fixing on getting somewhere very fast. It sounds much better to say that this is a battle we have won. Or that at the very least, it's an enemy we've got the drop on. Like the man who tells his doctor, "I'm learning how to relax—but I want to relax better and faster. I want to be on the cutting edge of relaxation!"

When the to-do list precedes the to-be list, distraction surely follows. But we have learned the art of staying one step ahead, haven't we? So we page. We fax. We phone. We e-mail. For we must hurry up. Get it done quick. Now is too late. Just do it.

Even the church is not exempt. Thomas Kelly, a Quaker theologian, warns churches that rely too easily on a "jitterbug program of fevered activities."

Which means that to be human in a world mesmerized by speed is a tough road. Precisely because it needs to be intentional. Which makes this a spiritual endeavor. For to be human is a matter of reclamation. Doris Grumbach writes about the reclamation in her book *The Presence of Absence,* where she talks about wanting to "document my own journey to slowing down." Stillness doesn't necessarily sell.

I had a conversation recently with someone wondering about my current project.

"What are you writing about now?" he asked.

"Slowing down," I answered.

"Slowing down?" As in, surely there's more.

"Yep. You know, learning to sit still."

"Sit still? Why?" As in, this man needs help. Serious help.

"It helps us to see."

"See what?"

"You know," I searched for words, "to see the world around us."

He scrunched his eyebrows and an invisible hook tugged up on the left side of his lip. "What on earth for?"

It's awfully tempting to segue into some kind of moral spitting contest, bragging about how some of us have a "less hectic lifestyle than the unfortunate others," and all the while our blood pressure rises, and the lesson is lost, degenerating into a battle not worth winning unless it's for bragging rights to fill some hole in the soul. Besides, I know where they're coming from. And this isn't about them. It's about me. And the crazy cultural mandate for busyness and speed that courses through my veins.

I've had my plate full of activity and distraction. Too full. So full it required periodic explanation and justification just to soothe my regret. And I complained. In a good natured way, of course. But who was I kidding. For some reason, it felt good, this need for pressing preoccupation.

"I've never been busier," I would tell whoever asked. Was it all for bragging rights?

"Busy? Are you kidding? It's nonstop." I reassured those who wondered. Did I look for surreptitious glances of envy?

"You know how it is. There's always something to be done. Maybe I'll find time this summer. Or next." I explained, during conversations about how our days—and lives—are slipping away. Was I not so sure that I could handle the alternative?

What was I hoping for, that all of my bluster and bravado (you know, life is busy, therefore I am) would impress the unseen judges of fate?

However you slice it, slowing down is a tough sell. But sooner or later, an essential one. I embraced the internal tapes that encouraged and promoted hell-bent pacing. And I lived my life as if I were indefinitely preparing to live.

"You can always slow down later on," was the justification. "What do you think retirement is for?" I guess the bottom line is that sooner or later, all of this activity-mania sours, at least it did for me. And I realized that I didn't like it, what it did to me deep down inside.

My friend and I go back and forth about all of this. He tells me that some people spend time to buy money. While others spend money to buy time. I confess that it takes me awhile to process this piece of wisdom. The part I do understand is that time is a commodity, a consumable not all that different from savings bonds.

By way of explanation, my friend tells me that I need to get a bigger, faster computer.

"Why?" I ask.

"You can go from application to application much quicker," he tells me. "It saves all kinds of time. How long does it take you now?"

"About thirty seconds," I answer.

"Well, there you have it. With a better machine it'll happen almost instantaneously," he informs me.

"How have I lived without all that extra time?" I ask in mock horror.

My friend calls me names. I told him that next time he can just e-mail his maledictions, it'll save him time.

I am still in the dark ages. I have a love-hate relationship with technology. I confess that this is no moral advantage. I've always been slow to jump on any bandwagon. It was no temptation for me to be one of the first to "get online." Truth is, it took a few years of cajoling from friends before I broke down and purchased a computer. So I've come that far. But I do not own a fax. Color me out-of-touch, or old fashioned, or just plain goofy.

It's not that I am opposed to gadgetry for the sake of opposition. You know, wandering around with a sandwich-board warning that technology is indeed the Anti-Christ.

But what fascinates me the most is that now with ubiquitous technology, everyone who needs anything from me wants it today. Or sooner. Now why on earth would that be? What follows is not an atypical telephone conversation with a client of mine, who absolutely *needs* something from me posthaste.

"I'll pop it in the mail," I tell him.

"What, are you kidding, that could take three or four days!" The alarm palpitates through the phone wires.

"Probably." I think I'll make him sweat.

"Well, it would be better if you faxed it to me." He is trying to sound polite.

"Good idea. Except that I don't have a fax."

"You don't have a fax?" He thinks I'm pulling his leg. There's a silence. Then, "You're serious, you don't own a fax? What are you, Amish?"

"Nope. I mean, there's one in town I can rent by the page." I don't tell him it costs an arm and a leg.

You can hear the sigh of relief. "Good. Why don't you go to town and fax the stuff to me. And hey, while you're at it, you need to get yourself a fax machine."

And, of course, off to town I will go. Either because I'm a nice guy, or I need the work. I never said that I would be consistent. But not before I get in one last shot, "Did it ever occur to you that maybe, just maybe, you need to call me three days earlier next time?"

And you hear the laughter, meaning "what a sense of humor, and isn't that a funny line." Which guarantees that I spend the first forty-five minutes in town running all my other errands—grocery, post office, bakery. Let 'em sit by their fax and wait. It'll give them something to do.

It's not that I have anything against a fax machine. I think that they are pretty amazing. But I am against the notion that somehow, because of machines, we are people of greater accomplishment, married to the illusion that we are therefore further ahead.

"Do you realize how much time you would save," one friend told me, in a tone part parent, part salesman.

"If it saves so much time," I tried my most unctuous tone, "why are you always needing things last minute?" There is more laughter, for apparently I'm the dense one here and the onus for time management (and hence, time's a-wasting) is on those of us unfortunate ones without the machines.

I do have one friend who has a cell phone. She carries it in her purse. But she has never tuned it on. I love it. I guess it's like an unloaded gun, something menacing to wave at the guilt-mongers.

Chances are, just like with my computer, some day I'll give in and have all the latest and most efficient gadgets. I guess my point is that it won't matter. Technology doesn't in and of itself change me. If I'm in a hurry now, I'll be in a hurry then. Doesn't take genius-level logic to factor that equation. Even so, there's something insidiously seductive about the toys. Not for the wealth of information available, or the new methods of communication, or even for the speed. The seduction works at the core of our being. Somehow, someway, I will be a new man.

It still comes back to facing the demon, doesn't it? That part of us unable to stop.

Embracing the pleasure of slowness

> "Why has the pleasure of slowness
>
> disappeared? Ah, where have they gone,
>
> the amblers of yesteryear? Where have
>
> they gone, those loafing heroes of folk song,
>
> those vagabonds who roam from one mill
>
> to another and bed down under the stars?
>
> . . . They are gazing at God's windows."
>
> Milan Kundera's

I like *Milan Kundera's* phrase "the pleasure of slowness." But here's the rub: Pleasure in slowness is not easy to find. Yes, slowing down reduces the noise. But slowing down goes hand in hand with stillness. And eventually, with silence. And in this culture, we seem undone by silence. Or we're leery at the very least. For silence, or so we are led to believe, is an unwelcome void. Even more, it is an indictment. Which means that to the enterprising western mindset, it is an invitation to get about the task of filling whatever it is that may be missing. Silence, it seems, provides us a ready-made market for some must-have, can't-miss, too-good-to-be-true product, designed to give us those hours of fun (or useful productivity) that we were apparently needing.

It all feels exaggerated by the assumption that such a space exists only because we were unable, lacking either creativity or industry, to find something to do. And we miss the point. For now, silence is the enemy, and any empty space, a weakness. Of what, I wonder, are we afraid? What is so comforting about noise? And what is the alternative we wish to avoid?

Perhaps this helps to explain our aversion to boredom, that great American antagonist.

"I'm bored," a mantra learned from early childhood.

"Can't you find something to do?" I can still hear my mother's voice.

Of course it is true that we are all wired a bit differently. Many of us are energized by respites of solitude—or quiet time—just sitting still. Before I give a lecture, I make it a point to find a secluded corner to sit, gather my thoughts, catch my breath, before I am "on." Invariably, someone will find me and ask in a voice of grave concern, "Are you okay?" There is a litany of others who pass by. "Is there something we can do for you?" "You don't need to be alone, you know." "Are you sure you're okay?" Five or six interruptions later, someone will ask, "Are you depressed or something?" By then the answer is certain, "Yes, come to think of it, I am."

Even with Mother Teresa's endorsement, "God is the friend of silence," it is not surprising that stillness can be unnerving. And it is not surprising that our perception of stillness (or solitude) has little chance for success, starting off as it does on such a wrong foot. With our eyes narrowed and our eyebrows furrowed, we stare stillness down, daring it to stay around and ruin our day.

We carry the same distaste for loneliness. Not that the two are synonymous. They certainly are not. But our attitude sure lumps them together. We treat loneliness as some sort of malady, an illness to be cured. Are you lonely? Then for God's sake, find somebody. Are you in a state of solitude? Are you undone by silence? Then by all means, get up and do something useful with your life.

But not even silence and solitude are synonymous. We can enjoy silence even in the company of others. In fact, sometimes it's a sign of health. Like my buddies Frog and Toad, who, in one of their stories, learned how to be best friends while sitting alone together. The Society of Friends (Quakers) makes silence an integral part of their worship service (called a gathering meeting) to let the dust settle (so to speak) and to let the imagination and insight rise. Thomas Kelly in *The Eternal Promise* defined true Quaker group worship as a special time

> . . . when an electric hush and solemnity
> and depth of power steals over the
> worshipers. A blanket of divine covering
> comes over the room, a stillness that can
> be felt is over all, and the worshipers are
> gathered into a unity and synthesis of
> life that is amazing indeed. A quickening
> Presence pervades us, breaking down some
> part of the special privacy and isolation of
> our individual lives.

And Lord knows there are times of solitude that are far from silent. On a visit to a secluded beach on the island of Kauai, I saw a person propped in a beach chair—alone for miles—serenaded by a boom box cranked up to dizzying decibels, looking for all intents and purposes like some poster child for irony.

Stillness as a healing sacred space

What's at stake here—with this sacred necessity of stillness—is not another to-do list, but an invitation to savor the pleasure of slowness, moments of stillness, even silence, letting them work their magic. In her book *The Solace of Open Spaces,* Gretel Ehrlich talks about the concept that space can heal. That space—created by silence—represents sanity. For silence can be a fullness, rather than a void. It can allow the mind to run through its paces without any need for justification. It can let us recover—grab hold of—those parts of our self which have been so scattered, so disparate, throughout the week. "We can make our minds so like still water that beings gather about us, that they may see their own images, and so live for a moment with a clearer, perhaps even a fiercer life, life because of our quiet," William Butler Yeats wrote. Or as a friend told me, "It feels like my life has been saved and I wasn't even aware of any danger. I see the stillness as a necessity, demandable, honorable. This is not sinful, or indulgent, or wasteful, or undeserved."

Silence can let the particulate (of daily nuisances) sift down to the bottom. Letting all that happen is a toxic flush-away. It fills our being with pure air, that blast of unadulterated oxygen straight to the head. It's all about what we can notice—and see—when we slow down and let the silence descend. It's about paying attention. Which is, novelist Jim Harrison used to say, the only game in town.

To sit still is a spiritual endeavor. To sit still is to practice Sabbath—meaning literally, to quit. To stop. To take a break. To make uncluttered time.

There is nothing holy or devout about the word Sabbath. It is about our basic need to quiet the internal noise. To separate ourselves from the people who cling to us. And to separate ourselves from the routines to which we cling.

At face value, it all sounds so essential, so inviting. But if that's the case, then why is it that in the real world stopping always feels like an interruption?

Routines are vital. My day is off to a bad start if I forgo my routine. So are deviations to the routine. Especially if they slow us down. A few months ago, I watched a squirrel have lunch. There is a family (or two) who live in the trees near our house, and they spend much of the day chattering and gossiping in a pinched and overwrought tone. They are careful to avoid any and all contact with our dogs—preferring to scold from on high.

Our doghouse is tucked under two towering hemlock trees. Evergreen huckleberry shrubs grow near the base of both trees and some branches hang over the roof. This little squirrel decided to push his luck, enter enemy territory, sit on top of the doghouse and have his lunch. He feasted on huckleberries. He would pull off one berry at a time using both hands, and fastidiously nibble away, his jaw the consistent motion of a miniature typewriter, all the while studying me out of the corner of his eye.

When he finished, I decided that since I was off schedule already, I'd walk through the garden.

In one little corner is a clump of autumn crocus. They generally bloom here in the Pacific Northwest beginning in late October and early November. Like their more popular springtime blooming relatives, these flowers stand three to five inches tall on single stems growing from a tuft of leaf blades. The fall crocuses in my garden are a pale lavender. The drawback is that they are not sturdy-stemmed. And excessive rain means flowers jackknifed back into the ground. Well, in this part of the world, excessive rain is common, which means that I haven't had an autumn pass without a puddle of contorted crocuses. Even so, I refuse to dig them up. When they first push their way through the soil, they look like a colony of upright nib pens. And I never remember that they are there until I see them each October. Invariably, during one of my autumn garden cleaning escapades, I come across this little patch of crocus, and it interrupts my work like a serendipitous treat. I can't help but giggle.

So I do what I must. I stop and put down my tools for a spell. I invite the stillness. It is my way of paying homage.

> Christopher Robin said, "What do you like doing best in the world, Pooh?"
>
> "Well," said Pooh, "what I like best"—and then he had to stop and think. . . . When he had thought it all out, he said, "What I like best in the whole world is me and Piglet going to see you, and you saying 'What about a little something?' and me saying, 'Well, I shouldn't mind a little something, should you, Piglet,' and it being a hummy sort of day outside, and birds singing."
>
> "I like that, too," said Christopher Robin, "but what I like doing best is nothing."
>
> "How do you do nothing?" asked Pooh, after he had wondered a long time.

"Well, its when people call out at you just as you're going off to do it, 'What are you going to do, Christopher Robin,' and you say, 'Oh, nothing,' and then you go and do it."

"Oh, I see," said Pooh.

"This is a nothing sort of thing that we're doing now."

"Oh, I see," said Pooh again.

"It means just going along, listening to all the things you can't hear, and not bothering."

"Oh!" said Pooh.

They walked on, thinking of this and that, and by-the-by they came to an enchanted place on the very top of the forest. . .

And by-the-by Christopher Robin came to an end of things, and was silent, and he sat there looking out over the world, and wishing it wouldn't stop.

"Nothing in all of creation is so godlike

as stillness."

        —Meister Eckhart

"Today I am going to pamper my soul."

   —Rabbi Zalman Schachter-Shalomi

"Grace is what happens when you are
face to face with acceptance without the
luxury of any justification."

4

When I moved to Vashon Island, I traded a townhouse in for an ample English-style house settled in the middle of acres of woodland, on an island in the Puget Sound. The house was built with old granite ballast stones reclaimed from decommissioned turn-of-the-century ships, and bulky cedar timbers milled from two grand old trees that had been already lying in the woodland. The townhouse I left was not altogether different from a hundred other stucco boxes cramped on meager suburban lots, scrolled through cul-de-sacs. Not altogether different from a myriad of adjacent cul-de-sacs strewn like small solar systems among millions of other solar systems that stretched on as far as the eye could see. My new house, by comparison, felt medieval and permanent.

Off the back of the house was a fair-sized patio made of the same ballast granite blocks, bordered by a stone wall. The wall was blanketed with the unpretentious canary yellow flowers of an unknown groundcover, as if the wall were draped in my grandmother's Sunday-go-to-meeting shawl. At the time I bought the house, I knew nothing of plants or plant names, blessedly inculpable, not caring that the charming groundcover was most ordinary, known by the unglamorous common name of 'creeping Jenny.' I also did not know when I bought the house that off the back patio were a fig tree, a plum tree, two cherry trees, and three apple trees. I did not know that the area adjacent to the pathway that led from the patio would be littered with the azure blooms of spanish bluebells each spring. I did not know that springtime would commence with a pyrotechnic display of blooms.

I know this: My heart skipped a beat as I explored the property, and that I did not tell anyone for fear of being misunderstood. I know that I was enthralled and I couldn't wait to walk the area behind the house in early morning when the grass was still burnished in heavy dew, and in the early evening when the light rendered everything in a lavender haze. I know that as I wandered, I discovered and daydreamed. Everything felt new and invigorating.

I know that all of this was a gift of grace. And I took possession of my life there. I became comfortable in my own skin.

I learned that the opposite of depression is not happiness, but delight. Grace fuels delight. Grace is that which tumbles into our lives, and we are spontaneously surprised by the goodness and beauty of living. C. S. Lewis called it "surprised by joy." Like the time I watched a pod of orca whales swim along the bow of the island ferry. I watched a mother and her calf stroll seamlessly through the water, their black and white markings looking like a rain slicker glistening in the sunlight.

Now, looking back, with the clarity of hindsight and solace from lessons learned, there is no reason I could not have discovered such moments of grace among the stucco box houses of my former life.

But that is precisely the point. I wasn't looking.

Neither was I looking when I moved north. Grace took me by surprise, when—for whatever reason—my defenses were relaxed.

The sacred necessity of grace

Grace is a sacred necessity because it takes root at the core of our being. To live "in grace" is to see differently. In grace, we move from an awareness of acceptance, not seeking or striving for acceptance. In grace, we no longer need to stay busy to impress.

But, we are either on the receiving end of grace, or we just flat out don't see it. Because it does no one any good to attempt to create it or duplicate it.

Grace comes to us. Like the birth of our son. Zachary Andrew Hershey slid, plunged, wrested his way into this world (our world) buoyed by the floating strains of the Tallis Scholars' rendition of Duarte Lobo's Requiem Mass, which is an altogether wonderfully peculiar hymn for a nativity; but given that there are no edicts precluding wake music at a birth, Zachary permeated our world as the lyrical chants wafted and permeated his birthing room. His mother labored—twenty and a half hours by my reckoning—to the voices of the Benedictine monks of Santo Domingo de Silos and the Tallis Scholars' lilting William Byrd's Three Masses. The air in the room was suffused with the essential oils of lavender and frankincense.

There was no need to scrimp here. This was indeed liturgy of the most high.

It took my emotions some lag time, and I can see, now, why the vessel—the surroundings, the ambience—for the birth is so essential, as it must hold the myriad of feelings, massaging and protecting them until later on, say, in the early hours of the next morning, when the carousel of memory and feeling are in sync. It hits you what you have just been through, and what it means to witness a miracle. And you hold your son and your wife, and feel a white-light stab of pure joy.

There are no rules here, and I felt the overwhelming reverberation, the import of this event, all of it churning in an inadequate container, and it is easy to be frustrated and baffled by a paucity of language, wondering how to express this joy for which there are no suitable vows. And all you can do is find a liturgy to hold it, to retain it for recall, to keep it holy—so utterly ordinary, so utterly extraordinary.

Our first morning home was a pristine winter day. By the time I began my walk there was no frost left on the neighbor's lawns, but the air was still crisp and pure. Near the top of the walk a pileated woodpecker announced my son's birth to the canyon, and his steady drumbeats on a fir tree-trunk echoed through the morning air. At the top of the drive, Mount Rainier stood off to the southeast in a smoky sheet of gauze.

There are two great enemies of grace

There are two great enemies of grace. One is the temptation to work for or earn it. So much so that we equate our very worth with work, and find ourselves missing those moments when the heavens have opened.

My friend Tim Hansel was writing a book on parenting. So he asked his two boys, "How do you know dad loves you?" He thought they'd say, "Dad, remember when you took us to Disney World for like ten days!" But they didn't say that. He thought they'd say, "Dad, remember Christmas and you bought us all that stuff!" They didn't say that either. They told him, "Dad, we know you love us when you wrestle with us."

He remembered two times when he had come home, he was late and tired and he didn't care, and these two urchins were jerking on his pant legs. He tells me, "So I rolled with them on the floor toward the kitchen, just to get them out of my way. And you know what," he continued the story, "in the middle of that very ordinary, very mundane experience, real life was happening. Real grace was happening. But I missed it, because I was only tuned in to Disney World and Christmas. There's nothing wrong with Disney World and Christmas, but grace is found in the wrestling times."

The other enemy is the feeling that we don't merit grace in the very least, and we go about our days stewing, living at a slow burn, raging at whomever, trying to decide when and where life dealt us the short straw. In the end, our energy is spent righting grievances and wrongs (whether perceived or real) until the balance sheet gives us some satisfaction that justice has been served, that we have received our due. Of course, the verdict comes many months or years down the road, well past the time we have forgotten the details that fueled our rage for so long. It kept us hot for years, but turns out to be an expensive use of fuel.

Annie Dillard weighs in on the subject of sulking in *Pilgrim at Tinker Creek*:

> Thomas Merton wrote, "There is always a temptation to diddle around in the contemplative life, making itsy-bitsy statues." There is always an enormous temptation in all of life to diddle around making itsy-bitsy friends, and meals, and journeys for itsy-bitsy years on end. It is so self-conscious, so apparently moral, simply to step aside from the gaps where the creeks and winds pour down, saying, I never merited this grace, quite rightly, and then to sulk along the rest of your days on the edge of rage. I won't have it. The world is wilder than that in all directions, more dangerous and bitter, more extravagant and bright. We are making hay when we should be making whoopee; we are raising tomatoes when we should be raising Cain, or Lazarus.

The bookkeepers who maintain office space in the back of our minds work overtime to keep us wired to the notion that public opinion and achievement count for something. And they conveniently point out that our shortcomings only serve to require more diligence in the endeavor.

I intended to write this week, but Penny, our fourteen-year-old golden retriever is at the end of her journey. So I was distracted. We returned home the other night to find her on the driveway, disoriented and unable to stand, unable to focus, her head bobbing and weaving with what looked like a seizure. The vet told us that it's not uncommon with dogs her age and that this may be the time, the circumstance, to let her rest in peace. Even so, we've given her some steroids and antibiotics on the slight chance that it's a temporary deal. "It's a quality of life decision," the vet told us, as we all hunched down on the floor of the veterinary office, petting Penny and reassuring her that someone was still there and that her world, as she knew it, had not completely abandoned her. "You know, is she still able to eat? Does she enjoy her food? Is she able to pee without discomfort and does she enjoy having people around her?" he asked us. And we said that she did. But how do you know?

This will be the second animal we've had to put down in the last few months. They do feel like markers, those events and circumstances that we use to gauge life's unyielding advance. The ones we remember and grieve and talk about as time goes by.

"Do you remember?"

"Has it been that long ago?"

"It just doesn't seem possible."

How easy it is, I thought hunched over in a veterinary office, letting the moment slip. So, we made the decision to keep Penny with us, for a few days more anyway. This morning she tried to go on her walk. It's an immutable morning custom, a two mile walk before breakfast. And it is, without question, the occasion that gives her the greatest joy. Today she stumbled out of the shed, hung over on unsteady legs, trying her best to carry on with life as she remembered it. We were surprised that she walked (well, wove and staggered, but her tail wagging the entire time) almost forty yards before she caved in, unable to continue. Even so, it was a good morning, as she washed her pill down with a canned dog food treat, her eyes still radiating joy.

"My favorite time of year is when my mom comes home."

—a young boy

Tell me, where does one go to find grace?

We have a choice. We can live life as a gift to be embraced and explored. Or, we can take the typical western worldview—treat everything like a test. It is the mental tic of our techno age. We look for solutions and gadgets. Moments of grace made to order, as if they can be orchestrated. This is one of the sticky wickets of landscaping. Some folks want a certain look and hope that with enough dollars the right people can be hired to pull it off. Grace, we tell ourselves, is like life—something to be managed, as if it were no different than pneumonia.

The Princess of Wales Memorial Fountain has opened in London's Hyde Park. It was meant to be more than a provocative piece of sculpture. The intention was that children would wade in it, race sticks down its watery lanes, and frolic about in its shallow pools.

Something went awry. After several accidents, people slipped and fell; the Parks Department panicked and quickly closed the fountain. A chain link fence was erected around the monument to keep the public from swarming in, guards were hired for wading-control purposes, and signs were posted setting out the new no-frolicking policy.

Is it possible to make space for something that stands over and against our hope for control? Where, pray tell, does one go for grace?

We will find a way, we tell ourselves. For we believe that it is only a matter of doing something, going somewhere, planning something, orchestrating events (as if in the orchestration we can make anything happen). Quality time with our children (my favorite book title, *One Minute Bedtime Stories,* for parents with little free time), leisure time, significant relationships, selling or negotiating, and scheduling our calendars all fall under the sway of this compulsion to manage. With enough information and forethought, we are certain that we can confiscate all.

Grace, it turns out, plays by different rules. Grace, it turns out, cannot be managed. For grace comes to us without pretense and often without warning. And grace asks only that we open ourselves—create a place somewhere inside—in order to receive it.

Our choice determines our path. Until and unless I give up life as a test, this sacred necessity will be unable to enter. Life as a test provides a frontline defense.

I was raised in church. I still have my perfect Sunday School attendance pins—thirteen years worth of perfect attendance— to prove it. However, to say that one was raised in the church does not mean one knows anything about grace. That is my experience. With my religious upbringing, God and grace soon diverge. I would hear the words (God and grace) in the same sentence but they rang hollow, intoned for public display, and contradictory to all experience.

From all indications, the God of the fundamentalist church treats grace like some second-tier motivational tool. The God of my upbringing was, above all else, holy. And plenty pissed off. Life is played out as if it's a big budget epic film with grand sound effects, casts of thousands, and a whole lot of smiting.

In the end, this God struck me as no different than an alcoholic father. A fragile ego propped up by capricious control. And all under his roof walked on eggshells, eager for any morsel of love or kindness, all the while waiting for the axe to fall . . .

I was taught (or more likely, ingested by osmosis) that playing the right notes trumped all else as a life goal. It is important that I look right to be right. The reality is that I am on duty, vigilant 24 / 7. And if we're lucky, something snaps. There is a crack in the façade, and the light of grace shines in.

"Judas come home. All is forgiven."

—graffiti on a public bathroom wall

There is a time when one slowly removes the armor worn to protect or impress

One could make the case that the sacred necessity is vulnerability. Or receptivity.

George Carlin does a great and telling riff about Americans and our stuff. That's what makes us Americans. We have stuff and take stuff with us when we go places. We buy more stuff and bring it home. And to appease our guilt, we set up a table in front of our home every summer and sell our stuff to our neighbors. And we walk around the neighborhood and buy their stuff at a bargain. We buy things we don't need with money we don't have to impress people we don't like.

Physical stuff. Mental stuff. Lives filled with stuff. Big fat stuff. Fat stuff from big fat stores filling fat houses, paid for with fat mortgages, fueling fat stress and temporarily assuaged by big fat food, consumed in a hurry.

There's a great story about a young man traveling Europe by train. At one border-crossing before an overnight ride he was advised, "Lately there has been a rash of theft, and we take no responsibility for your personal belongings." Well, that'll make you nervous. So, he did what anxious people do. He stayed awake, staring at his stuff. Finally, at two in the morning, he drifted off to sleep. After twenty minutes, he awoke with a start, looked at the luggage rack and saw that his stuff was gone. "Thank God," he said, "Now I can sleep."

One day it hits you: This is a lot of energy to impress some unseen table of judges. Instead of seeking to be original, I've spent my life working to be cool, accepted. Afraid of being beautiful in my own way, I strive to look like the latest version of "Extreme Makeover."

I stewed and moaned in the ferry line. Stewing and moaning can be a rewarding and full time occupation in the sodden world of the Northwest. You know the storyline. It rains a lot here. The sky is gunmetal gray. Our mood is a corresponding gray. This color stains our psyche some deep shade of indigo and we battle claustrophobia. But I digress, and you may already see my point that there is very little upside to this line of reasoning.

We board the ferry and head west toward our island. Spring here, as in many parts of our world, is marked by volatile skies and sudden weather changes.

What a remarkable drama on this afternoon. The skylights were dimmed as if on cue, now auditorium lights, readied for a performance. Directly over Vashon Island—stretching sixteen to twenty miles—a cloud formation hovers. It is dense and backlit, a solid configuration not quite yet identifiable, perhaps the beginning of an immense marble statuary. As if the island were a pedestal where the statue was to be set down.

I walk out to the railing on the ferry's upper deck to witness. Between the island and the ferry, the Puget Sound is an angry blue, vexed with white caps. The gods of the sea are embroiled. The wind is bracing against my face. The music of the sky and sea is bold and dramatic. Tchaikovsky, not Chopin.

In a matter of minutes, great shafts of sunlight surge down upon and over the island. As if the cloud formation had rent, the bottom torn from the weight, all of its contents poured out, emptied.

And then, just as suddenly, the drama is over.

Now empty, the formation breaks apart and dissipates into a collection of innocuous cloud shapes, sliding through the skies.

I stay by the railing. But there is no encore.

I want to cheer.

Instead, I stand in silence, surrounded by the sacredness of life. And the voice of grace. And I see and hear it clearly. In the words of Dag Hammarskjold:

> **Thou**
> **Whom I do not know**
> **But whose I am.**

The most beautiful things in the world are the most useless

There is no balance sheet for any of this. And it brings to mind John Ruskin's reminder (back in 1853) that "the most beautiful things in the world are the most useless; peacocks and lilies for instance." But useless is a tough sell in today's market. Try this: The next time you go into a bookstore, go to the counter and ask for a book that has seven strategies for a useless day.

Henri Nouwen, Roman Catholic theologian, pushes the envelope when he talks about the fact that we must intentionally learn how to be "useless." This is an odd word to our North American sensibilities. Sitting still, we realize that life is not a beauty pageant, or a race, or a contest. For then and only then do we know that our identity is not dependent on what we do, or how we look, or what we've accomplished, or whom we know.

In his book, *Lifesigns,* Nouwen talks about the time spent at *l'Arche,* a home for mentally handicapped adults in France. He observes:

> **While the needs of the world clamor for our attention, hundreds of capable, intelligent men and women spend their time, often all of their time, feeding broken people, helping them walk, just being with them, and giving them the small comfort of a loving word, a gentle touch, or an encouraging smile. To anyone trying to succeed in our society, which is oriented toward efficiency and control, these people are wasting their time. What they do is highly inefficient, unsuccessful, and even useless.**

Now there's a thought. We literally find the love of God—the fullness of God—in these "useless" moments.

Tonight there is a full moon. I see it in the southern sky through the trees. The tips of several leafless alder trees are backlit and appear etched. I squint my eyes and the child in me is in full throttle. I can see ET riding his bike—against the moon—through the sky. The clock stops in these moments. And we take with us something that sustains us for days, maybe even for months, or for a good lot longer than that. We literally honor life.

> Sabbath implies a willingness to be surprised
> by unexpected grace, to partake of those
> potent moments when creation renews
> itself, when what is finished inevitably
> recedes, and the sacred forces of healing
> astonish us with the unending promise of
> love and life.

> —E. L. Doctorow

If we live in grace, we pay attention

Each of the sacred necessities have this in common: paying attention. But, as Simone Weil has pointed out, there is all the difference in the world between real attention, which has to do with waiting, emptying your mind, expectant and receptive, and a kind of misdirected muscular effort.

> If one says to one's pupils: "Now you must
> pay attention," one sees them contracting
> their brows, holding their breath, stiffening
> their muscles. If after two minutes they
> are asked what they have been paying
> attention to, they cannot reply. They have
> been concentrating on nothing. They have
> not been paying attention. They have been
> contracting their muscles.

There's talk about a need for change. But here's the bottom line: We can't change anything until we love it. We can't love anything until we know it. We can't know anything until we embrace it.

In a culture that places a premium on control, grace seems, surely, like madness. Random acts of madness.

I can tell you that when I listen to the voice of grace, I relax. I give up my need for control. I pause to relish the notion. And I can tell you that when I do pause, I begin to hear the voice of grace around me. I can tell you that this time of year the sun lingers in the southwestern sky just enough to make a difference. And that on a day like today, that difference takes you by surprise. Today the air smells of spring, the earth exudes warmth. So I remove my coat, and shake my head in disbelief. Off to my left, the miniature narcissuses are in full bloom, *tete-a-tete*. The forsythias have the spring stage to themselves, and the yellow appears backlit, an electrical neon, bold and unapologetic, making no attempt to blend in. There is little else to evaluate, so I lean back on the deck chair and drink it in, and a weight is gone, somehow lifted.

"Gardening is an instrument of grace."

—May Sarton

Simplicity

If thee needs

anything and cannot

find it,

just come to me

and I'll tell thee

how to get along

without it.

—Etta May (Quaker)

5

There were no gentle increments. No warning signs. No intervening calm. Winter blundered in, awkward and disruptive, out of the north, towing fat snowflakes, as if strung on horizontal wires. The temperature hovered at 32 or just above, so the snow fell wet, heavy, and iced. In the space of twenty minutes, everything was shadowed, outlined, or completely covered.

After an hour or more of snow and wind, the lights in our house flickered, and our electricity quit—which is not all that uncommon in this neck of the woods, so it didn't worry us any. But that day was different. We didn't know it at the time, but no one on the island had electricity, and our little town was for all intents and purposes shut down, as if one lone generator decided it had had enough, weary from well doing, and the hum of power simply gave up the ghost. We don't need much snow to shut down the roads here in the Northwest, and it looked like this storm would surely oblige, so we knew right off that schools would be closed, kids would be looking for sled runs, and most adults would be taking the day off from work.

My wife and I sat bundled up, sipping tea in our living room, watching the storm lash. The canyon—beyond our windows to the north—was completely fogged in, layered in clouds, so that we could not see the water of Puget Sound. Apparitions of hemlock and fir swayed in the fog.

We listened to the sounds, bursts of wind slaloming through the trees, an occasional crack followed by what sounded like the echoing report of a deer rifle shot as a branch somewhere in the canyon succumbed to the obdurate weight of the icy snow. As the moments of an intervening and edgy silence grew, I felt unnerved. For whatever reason, it is always a surprise, this absence—no familiar hum of electricity, heater fan, or background music. On that day, there were only the sounds of pencil on paper and the creaks and groans of our house. The rest of the world drifted away in silence. Any productive plans for that day were assuredly derailed. And, since I didn't own a sled, I settled for the next best option, curling up on the couch to finish a book.

By noon, the storm had not abated, and there were ten inches or more of snow, with the temperature still hovering at 32 degrees. I couldn't help but smile at this great blast of snow which hardly even qualified as a minor inconvenience—let alone a storm—to anyone from the Midwest or Northeast. Even so, I looked out the study window, worrying for the great madrone tree near the back of our lower garden. Well over 130 feet tall, forming a canopy of thirty to forty feet, the madrone's evergreen limbs were alarmingly bowed, like a fatigued heavyweight fighter who looks beaten, uncertain if he can go even one more round.

After lunch, my wife and I walked our dogs through the canyon. I would stop every few minutes, mesmerized by the cloak of quiet from this snow ladened world, watching the dogs who frolicked unabashedly in the drifts, captivated by their good fortune. I envied their unencumbered bliss. They knew the truth: If we do not bring it with us, we will not find it here.

Even so, we nurse those pictures in the back of our minds. Just in case. The beach house near Cabo San Lucas. The farmhouse in the Tuscan hills, with vineyard and fields of rosemary.

This life does not have a fighting chance against the promises of another life. In the battle waged in our minds, we find no place in our daydreams for the burden of being ourselves, where we are obliged—or is it blessed?—to be conscious. When we choose to live awake and aware, we give up the promises of another life. We learn to practice the art of wanting what we already have.

The sacred necessity of simplicity says, "enough is enough."

All too often, the mantra of "not enough" carries the day, and becomes the *de facto* setting for all our thinking and internal wiring. Since we are reminded—three thousand times a day—of what we should do, buy, or be, we assume that we must not have enough. We capitulate to public opinion. After all, "what would they think?"

There is a fundamental difference in paradigm. Simplicity argues from the paradigm of sufficiency. The alternative is to believe in, to be motivated by the poser of scarcity. With scarcity our hurried life is fueled by envy, competition, striving, and a need for control, and in the end becomes a justification for an unfulfilled life.

But what if who we are and what we have is sufficient? It would mean that we could choose to live by the sacred necessity of simplicity: sufficiency, living in gratitude, trust, respect, wholeness, and responsibility.

I'll practice simplicity after I'm happy

When writers gather, for whatever reason—sipping coffee, nursing beers, debating in writers' groups, or gossiping over the back fence—sooner or later the subject of writer's block hangs ominously, both familiar and unwanted.

"Are you writing?" my friend will ask, just trying to be friendly.

"Not lately," I have told him on more than one occasion.

It is what I say when I have writer's block. I heard one good writer say that writer's block is just poppycock. And he's right, of course. I mean, writing is just a job, and sitting before a blank screen or pad comes with the territory. You simply work through it. You just do. Even so, call it what you will, there are times when a sense of uselessness reaches around and sucker punches you when you least expect it. And while it is a condition without the social stigma of hemorrhoids, you're still prone to avert your eyes, as it carries, nonetheless, the shame of some personal shortcoming. As if it is something

I must apologize for. It is, to be sure, a piece of news best whispered among close friends.

"Are you okay?"

"Not really. It's writer's block, I'm afraid."

"Oh my," in a voice of genuine alarm, "how can you live another day?"

Such worries make sense when you recognize that writer's block is assumed to be, above all else, a waste of valuable time. If I'm not writing, then it goes without saying that I am not generating copy. And if I am not generating copy, then it goes without saying that I am not making my deadlines. And if I am not making my deadlines, then it goes without saying that somebody is going to be very, very unhappy. And it doesn't really matter who that somebody is. As long as there is unhappiness, and it is attributed to me, you can bet the farm that I feel responsible. And that, as they say, can mess up an otherwise halfway decent day.

What a double-whammied web to weave! Not only am I wasting time, but I'm also ruining someone else's day. I had no idea the extent of my power.

Like a golfer with the shanks, we writers are susceptible to any and every stratagem or apparatus which promises relief: everything from writing drills to breathing exercises to intensive weekend conferences convened at mountain hideaways, satiated with self-hypnosis, herbal tea, and group hugs. We are susceptible to anything that may relieve us from the indignity of having to admit that we are, for all intents and purposes, wasting our whole entire life! It doesn't occur to us—until, say, two years down the road—that exaggeration is an irritating side effect to our affliction/vocation.

In my experience, this is the way it all unfolds: I start to feel bad about myself, a little blue. Well heck, a lot blue. Say, some deep shade of murky indigo. Okay, maybe I've become a poster-child for Prozac. This funk, in turn, does a great deal for my motivation to write. Which means that I don't write. As in *nada*. Zero. I just turn on the computer and stare at the blank screen for as long as I can stand it, before I get up and walk around the house, room to room, rearranging books and chairs and whatever else that can occupy my mind and time for awhile. I end up back at the computer where the screen is still blank, where no miracle has taken place, no chapter has spontaneously appeared. By this time my head aches, which is a good enough reason to call it a day and make lunch. The fact that it is only nine-thirty in the morning is irrelevant.

It seems that the ones who are telling us how to get out of this quicksand are always standing comfortably on the solid ground of productivity. That is the curious thing about those times when we are writing along without a hitch in our giddy-up. We just can't believe that writer's block was ever a problem.

It's a battle, of course, we are destined never to win. In fact, never even to come close. Especially with the way we have defined success. To be a successful writer is to be a productive writer. To produce means to generate words on the page, which in turn means to get published and purchased. The more the merrier. A blank page is, above all else, a glaring indictment.

Apparently it's in our DNA, we just hate to waste time, as it calls into question our very vocation. And so begins the internal interrogation, "What in the world made you think you were a writer in the first place?"

Every vocation has a similar dynamic. It's all about productivity—getting more done, moving up, making more so we can have more.

This full-court press filled with advertising promises for a better life leaves no one unscathed. So much for simplicity. I tell myself that I'll practice simplicity after I am happy.

The hook of this advertising crusade is predicated on our embracing this notion of scarcity. Lynne Twist, in an insightful book entitled *The Soul of Money,* offers a revealing glimpse of how far into our souls the tendrils of acquisitiveness have reached:

> **My friend Janie was visiting the home of an old potter at Santa Clara pueblo. She was admiring the enormous collection of pots her host had on display throughout his home. "How many do you have?" my friend innocently inquired. Her host lowered his eyes. "We do not count such things," he replied quietly.**

The whole internal drama brings to mind the plant *Campanula rapuncuoides.* (When you are a gardener, everything reminds you of a plant. It is an occupational malady.) At any rate, *C. rapuncuoides* is a dastardly, invasive plant with charming lavender bells on medium height stems. And no landscape is safe from its galloping runners. Dig it up if you will. But any of the slightest slivers of roots left in the soil will become, by next year, a full grown plant with malice aforethought. If you thought the Norman Conquest was brutal, well . . . try this genteel little dandy in your flower bed.

This promise of "another life" is forged of the very same heart and pith. Dig it up if you will, only to discover that slivers of the contagion have commandeered crevasses in your psyche, where they happily root and taunt and thrive.

And yet we continue to dig. In our hearts we see scarcity as a fixable problem.

Help is on the way. I read recently that one can rent a wife. Really. Not that this surprises me. I take my hat off. For whoever created such an enterprise has an entrepreneurial flair. Not to mention a fair notion about what ails us all. Out of breath and out of time, what's a few bucks to get us back on track?

With rent-a-wife, you can hire someone to pick up your dry cleaning. Do your laundry. Run your errands. Drop your kids off at school (or day care). And then pick them up after school if necessary. A rent-a-wife will shop for your groceries and make out your weekly menus. (I read no mention of a rent-a-husband option. Apparently not as popular, they just sit on the couch clutching the remote control.)

There's another company that will cook your meals. They can even do a week's worth of meals in advance, storing them all in the freezer with labels. All you need is a microwave. It's the next best thing to a live-in cook.

Still another business will send care packages to your kids while they are at camp. Not just any packages mind you, but packages "which look as if they came from you, but are in fact more skillfully targeted to current kid tastes." I see. Apparently the competition surrounding camp care packages is stiff. And we don't want to jeopardize our child's self-esteem with a less than satisfactory care package. But then, I must be out of touch. Either that, or I'm not too enthusiastic about ponying up the money just so my kid can win the package-most-envied award.

I read that the woman who started this rent-a-wife venture ran an ad that read simply, "BUY TIME." Now I know why she is a success. We are a culture voracious for time saving devises. Virtually every television infomercial promises that you will either lose weight or save time. Many promise to do both. If you can't afford to rent a wife, there are machines that will cook your meals faster. There are books that allow you to squeeze another hour out of the day. There are computers that send your e-mail messages virtually faster than you can write them. But my favorite is a two-hour seminar entitled, "Organize Your Child, Organize Yourself." These life organizers hit you in the soft spots.

Children get it right, the sacred necessity of simplicity

When my son was a toddler, we went for walks. I pushed his stroller (the jogging variety with bicycle wheels, although in truth, I have never actually jogged behind the stroller). Some mornings Zachary was game, even eager. But on others he preferred to read or play or dillydally. Then there is the perfunctory dressing dance that comes with winter weather. Coats and hats and boots. All put on while we're moving along the floor exploring and playing. It's a fifteen-minute episode, give or take ten minutes. This particular morning he's not being helpful. I start out polite, with suggestions about how much fun the walk would be if we were actually out walking, instead of scooting along the floor doing a square dance with our boots. He's not rising to the bait of courtesy. So I threaten him with the seminar, "If you keep this up, I intend to spend hard earned money learning how to organize you."

Finally, he's in the buggy. The rain cover is in place. And we're moving down the driveway. I have only one objective in mind: finish our two-mile walk as quickly as possible, especially now that we are running late. On our way down the driveway through our canyon, Zachary points, pleading with me to stop, in order to notice the filigreed fronds suspended from the trunk of a large maple tree. He points, "Wait. Look Dad. See. Licorice fern."

The sacred necessity of simplicity.

What we knew as children instinctively—life in its simple particularity—we lose as we move to adulthood and its fix-it society. This means that the appearance of "doing something" is crucial. Every problem has a solution and every dysfunction a protocol repair order. Read this or that book. Attend this or that workshop. Take this or that pill. Go on this or that cruise. Think this or that happy thought. And buy this or that "never before seen until this TV infomercial" solve-it gizmo. As if the conundrum of our dysfunction wasn't enough, now we have the pressure of a test on the power of our resolve.

I've never been shy with advice. So if I'm asked the "what should I do with my life" question, I give my one and only recommendation: *learn to pay attention.*

There is a domino affect:

Notice.

See.

Contemplate.

Relish.

Savor.

My bit of counsel is not all that popular and may explain why it is that I'm not asked for my two cents all that much. Even so, this advice is worth repeating: *learn to pay attention.*

When we pay attention, we arrest our need for perpetual motion (in the words of Tennessee Williams, "attempting to find in motion what was lost in space"). When we sit still long enough to pay attention, we allow all the parts of our hurried and fractured self to settle and congeal, and it reminds us that our worth has little to do with our pace or our productivity. There is no need to be king of the mountain. In this moment, it allows me to stop my writing and to watch the sun rays filter through the cedar trees near the garden, as drops from last night's rain glisten, revealing branches of jewels, and what is left of the morning fog slowly retreats into the woodland.

Have yourself a good, long, restful nothing

Pascal went so far as to suggest that "all of man's unhappiness stems from a single cause, his inability to remain quietly in a room." As in sit still the prerequisite for paying attention, in order to embrace that which is sufficient about our life: this life, this moment, this self. This makes some people downright nervous, myself included. It goes without saying that not everyone agrees with Pascal. As if he is implying that wholeness is linked to time spent in seclusion. For sitting still, however you slice it, conjures unpleasant images. We think of hermits in their solitude—who strike us as men or women just slightly off-plumb—sequestered away for the love of God and the need for self-flagellation; or we think of older, lonely widows puttering around the house, trying to put a more positive spin on their lot in life. In this culture, sitting still is solitary confinement . . . plain and simple.

In a posthumous collection of his works, *Anatomy of Restlessness,* the British travel writer Bruce Chatwin argues what he considers to be the alternative. He says that Pascal made that remark in one of his gloomier moments. We don't need sitting still, urges Chatwin, we need:

> **Diversion. Distraction. Fantasy. Change
> of fashion, food, love, and landscape. We
> need them as the air we breathe. Without
> change our brains and bodies rot. The man
> who sits quietly in a shuttered room is likely**

to be mad, tortured by hallucinations and introspection.

Chatwin goes on with his argument:

> Some American brain specialist took
> encephalograph readings of travelers.
> They found that changes of scenery and
> awareness of the passage of seasons through
> the year stimulated the rhythms of the
> brain, contributing to a sense of well-being
> and an active purpose in life. Monotonous
> surroundings and tedious regular activities
> wove patterns which produced fatigue,
> nervous disorders, apathy, self-disgust, and
> violent reactions. Hardly surprising, then,
> that a generation cushioned from the cold
> by central heating, from the heat by air-
> conditioning, carted in aseptic transports
> from one identical house or hotel to
> another, should feel the need for journeys of
> mind or body, for pep pills or tranquilizers,
> or for the cathartic journeys of sex, music,
> and dance. We spend far too much time in
> shuttered rooms.

Well, he's preaching to the choir. My grandfather's a great example. He worked his whole life, starting at age ten in the vegetable fields of north Florida for ten cents a day, until his retirement at age sixty-three. He loved to fish, and would take two or three trips a year with friends or grandchildren. Retirement would enable him to travel, to fish to his heart's content, in all the places he had dreamed about. It was the promise of that other life—that retirement life—which sustained him.

After he retired, my grandfather never fished. Not once. He sat in his rocking chair on his screened-in porch, and stewed: about the weather, about the economy, about my grandmother's health. Silence was not a respite for him, but a stockade.

So Chatwin's got no argument from me. There is, however, a significant difference. We must not assume that slowing down or stopping or embracing silence to pay attention is synonymous with confinement. Travel and confinement are hardly the opposite ends of a continuum. I, for one, am in favor of travel. I require it. It allows me to see, absorb, and learn. But isn't that the point? That one can find the same trap on the road. Of what use are travel, adventure, and exploration, when wherever we go, there we are in what Chatwin calls "a monotonous capitalistic sameness of product, landscape, and utter anonymity of place." Which is another way of saying that you can only see the same strip mall so many times before the air your brain needs begins to leech out of your reserve tank.

Take my trip to Las Vegas as evidence. It was a business trip, and my wife and I had a room in one of the larger casino hotels. It's easy to demonize the glitz and kitsch. But then, it's not everywhere that you can be married by Elvis. Yes, we know that it is an artificial world, one that attracts millions of visitors each year, for entertainment and distraction.

I will say this. I was never once alone. Literally. I mean that I was never in a place where I could catch my breath as it were, or my thoughts. There was no place where I could reflect or cogitate. There was no place where I wasn't bombarded by din, lights, and clamor. But then, that's the idea. After all, what kind of fun is it without din, lights, and clamor, the sure-fire recipe for revelry.

They have a time, say once a year at the Fat Tuesday Parade, that time when you throw all caution to the wind, say "the hell with it," and party without any pre-meditation in the vicinity. Whatever cleanup needs to be done can wait until tomorrow. But this wasn't Fat Tuesday, I was woeful at blackjack, and I had a headache.

Sometimes nature takes us by the hand to teach us the power of simplicity. On the last day of our trip, we drove west on State Road 159 toward the Red Rock Canyon Recreation Area. In Las Vegas proper, surrounded by inexhaustible glass and relentless fountains and gemstone green fairways, you can forget for a moment that you are, in fact, in the middle of a vast desert—one that stretches for miles and miles and miles. What a wasteland. What an astonishing wasteland.

You see Red Rock Canyon long before you arrive. You can't help but see it, as it rises abruptly above the desert floor, a formation of odd and unquestionable beauty. Somewhere in the neighborhood of sixty-five million years ago, two plates in the earth collided, and a mass of red sandstone ended up sandwiched in between two equally sized masses of military-camouflage-tan tinted stone. Such a marvel is caused when a fracture in the earth's crust drives one crustal plate over the top of another. The result is that the stone above is older than the stone below. As you begin to drive what is called the "scenic loop," before you find a place to park and explore, you notice that the car has dramatically slowed, as if of its own volition, and you wonder if the air is drugged. You feel the need to dawdle, to say nothing, but simply to stare and gape in awe. There is the illusion that time has slowed here, receded even, as if history's carousel had been ratcheted back a couple of notches. When you step out of your car, you momentarily forget where you are. It is the scale of the place, not merely its size, but its grandeur that strikes you. And whatever distractions you brought with you begin to fall away, as all of your energy is marshaled into absorbing whatever is around you. You feel the power of the natural world, as it absorbs the poison in you.

We walked and sat and looked and pointed. We watched families clamber around the sandstone formations—rounded and weathered smooth—the children laughing and waving to their parents below. Some folks were sitting alone. There were artists painting, adults snoozing on blankets perched on the rocks, and a few just standing and staring. Life—this life—took center stage.

You don't spend your hours pulling on slot machine arms here. On the strip, I watched families stopping to pose for pictures in front of casinos, limousines, and Disneyesque attractions. Twenty miles away, here in Red Rock Canyon, there is silence, save for the stream that runs down through the cathedral of primeval stone. And I wonder what happened to us.

No. I wonder what happened to me. I was spending the day at Red Rock only because my original plans didn't work out. I had intended to play golf, but didn't have a tee time, and the wait was much too long for a man with an agenda. The result of this fortuitous glitch in the schedule was, in the words of a Jim Harrison heroine, " a very long and restful nothing."

The sacred necessity of simplicity. Enough is enough.

Flunking my Sabbath is not such a bad notion

When I lived in Southern California, I spent two or three days every six weeks retreating at St. Andrew's Abbey. I went to St. Andrew's because I wanted to practice the art of sitting still. Thomas Kelly writes that "deep within us all there is an amazing inner sanctuary of the soul, a holy place, a Divine Center, a speaking Voice, to which we many continuously return." I wanted to find that place. And I wanted to learn how to be alone with me and like it, because I wasn't very good at that, for I still was consumed by the paradigm of scarcity (never enough, striving, competition). It is no wonder that I perceived and evaluated myself by measuring motion and activity. I had swallowed—hook, line, and sinker—the cultural imperative that I would be graded by how busy I could be with matters of consequence, which meant being on the right vocational track and climbing the right ladder. In response, I received adulation, the affirmation that I too indeed was busy, and therefore, important.

The only problem is that I didn't much care for the surcharge. I was living my days red-faced and anxious.

On my first weekend at St. Andrews, I had high hopes. I was going to slow down, catch my breath, return to my hectic world rejuvenated. I had made plans for a forty-eight-hour Sabbath—in the Hebrew sense of the word, which implies a time and space of nothing, or a hallowed waste of time. So off I went, armed with books to read and sermons to write. I charged into the weekend. This, as Sabbaths go, was going to be enormously and satisfyingly productive.

In *The Solace of Open Spaces,* Gretel Ehrlich tells it straight:

> We Americans are great on fillers, as if what we have, what we are, is not enough. We have a cultural tendency toward denial, but, being affluent, we strangle ourselves with what we can buy. We have only to look at the houses we build to see how we build against space, the way we drink against pain and loneliness. We fill up space as if it were a pie shell, with things whose opacity further obstructs our ability to see what is already there.

At lunch I had a conversation with Father Francis, my spiritual director, and told him of my high hopes. He made no attempt to dissuade me.

frolicked in the woods, hid in the forest, and acted silly. We laughed a lot.

Then, one day, this snake told us that we weren't having real fun, because we weren't keeping score. "Fun, like everything else in life," the snake told us, "needs to be a real matter of consequence." After he explained it, we still couldn't see the fun. But he said that we should give an apple to the person who was the best at playing, and we'd never know who was best unless we kept score. Now we could all see the fun of that. We were all sure we were the best at something.

It was different after that. We yelled a lot. We had to make up new scoring rules for most of the games we played. Other games, like frolicking, we had to stop playing, because how do you keep score when you frolic?

By the time God found out about our new fun, we were spending about forty-five minutes a day playing and the rest of the time working out the score. God was wroth about that, very, very wroth. He said we couldn't use his garden any more because we weren't having any fun. We said we were having lots of fun and he shouldn't have gotten so upset just because it wasn't exactly the kind of fun he had had in mind. He wouldn't listen. He kicked us out and said we couldn't come back until we stopped keeping score. To rub it in, and to get our attention, he told us that we were going to die anyway, and our scores wouldn't matter!

Well. He was wrong. Because my cumulative all game score is now 16,548 and that means a lot to me. And I figure if I can raise it to about 20,000 points before I die, I'll know I have

accomplished something. Even if I can't, my life has a great deal of meaning because I'm teaching my children to score high, and they should be able to reach 30,000 points. I mean fun is great in its place, but without scoring, there's no reason for it. God must have a very superficial view of life.

Or this one.

Mulla Nasrudin was eating a poor man's diet of chickpeas and bread. His neighbor, who also claimed to be a wise man, was living in a grand house and dining upon sumptuous meals provided by the emperor himself.

His neighbor told Nasrudin, "If only you would learn to flatter the emperor and be subservient, as I do, you would not have to live on chickpeas and bread."

Nasrudin replied, "And if only you would learn to live on chickpeas and bread, as I do, you would not have to flatter and live subservient to the emperor."

This is the way the parables translate to my life.

Today isn't a writer's blank-screen-day. I guess that means that I may be productive. Lucky me. Won't that impress the unseen panel of judges hovering just over my shoulder?

But truth is ironic. In the middle of my flurried "productivity," I heard the wind whipping around outside my study window. I glanced, just in time to see a pair of bald eagles, hovering right above the back deck, maybe thirty-five feet off the ground. One had landed in a towering fir a stone's throw away. The other eagle was close enough that I could hear the whoosh-whoosh of its great wings.

The pair were playing today. Letting the currents take and fling them. Letting the wind lead. Their calendar apparently had no other agenda. I watched for as long as I could follow them out through the canyon.

Then I had to wait for my heart to calm down before I could write another word.

After our big winter storm, several trees were down around the property. Alders (a weak tree, susceptible to wind and heavy snow) were snapped half or three-quarters of the way up, as if victims of some bizarre epidemic of flora osteoporosis. Some were uprooted, leaning onto other trees, looking like the aftermath of a battle with the healthy shouldering the wounded back to safety. Large limbs from fir and hemlock lay on the ground, snapped from the weight of the snow.

Our driveway was blocked by fallen trees in three places. But there was no rush, as we had nowhere to go, and no way to get there. So my wife and I worked through the afternoon, chainsawing, lopping, and limbing. Cutting wood was, hands down, a job I hated as a boy. My childhood home was heated by a bulky wood-burning furnace—our sole source of heat—and we consumed what appeared to me to be a Himalayan sized mound of wood any given winter. Which meant that every winter weekend, regardless of the weather or the temperature, we (my father, my younger brother, and I) would be (as in, no arguing, no voting, no option, no feigning sickness or death) somewhere in one of the local woodlands, cutting wood to maintain our mountain range reserve, stacked and curing for the next winter. By twelve I was splitting all sizes of wood rounds—I remember the mastery I felt from an accurate swing of the axe, splitting the log cleanly into two mirrored halves. (It was a skill spurred on in order to avoid my father's impatient, "What the hell are you doing? Can't you see which way the grain runs?") My father always assumed that the truck would hold more wood than I, which meant enduring the cold for thirty minutes longer than the three hours we had already been there.

While throwing wood into the truck bed, with my wool cap pulled down over my ears, I found ways to pass the time, retelling stories from Zane Grey or Robert Louis Stevenson in my mind, or sneaking an occasional snowball toss toward a tree ten yards away, where a batter stood with a full count and I needed only one more strike to end the ball game. Finally, at home, after we had unloaded and stacked the wood, I would bolt toward the large floor register in the kitchen, where I would claim squatter's rights, letting the heat blast my frozen fingers and toes. It was my first taste of a drug, this strange fusion of euphoria and torment, this fine line between relief and sharp pain, as if needles danced across my skin. Yes, it hurt, but I was in heaven, and wouldn't move until I was commanded to the table for supper.

Back in our canyon, the downed trees had been cut, chopped and stacked. With the chainsawing stopped, the contrast felt palpable. For a minute or so, there was absolutely no noise. So we stood for a while, under a canopy of hemlock and cedar. We began to walk home, and could hear only our own breathing, and the sound of our boots in the woodland snow.

"I always wanted to be somebody. I just

should have been more specific."

—Lily Tomlin

Resilience

"The earth is resilient. As creative beings, we, too, are resilient. We are watered by the slightest daily practice that brings our creativity gently to bloom."

—Julia Cameron

6

There's a haunting little memoir entitled *The Diving Bell and the Butterfly*, the story of Jean-Dominique Bauby, former editor of the French fashion magazine *Elle*. At the age of forty-three, Jean-Dominique suffered a rare kind of stroke to the brain stem. He awoke after twenty days in a coma. Only his left eye functioned. But his mind was unimpaired, frozen in a body which had but one meager way to communicate. It's the story about what it is like to be locked up, a prisoner in your own skin. I cannot imagine the terror, the claustrophobia. It is one thing to feel misunderstood. It is quite another to have utterly no recourse. To feel completely at the mercy of your body, medical and personal opinion, the good will of friends and acquaintances, and above all else, silence. In this case, the indictment of silence.

It was in that world that Bauby learned to probe inlets of sanity, or as he called them, the "only windows to my cell." To fall prey to daydreams of walking and talking. To find the "hours drag on but the months flash by." And then this:

> **Far from such din, when blessed silence returns, I can listen to the butterflies that flitter inside my head. To hear them, one must be calm and pay close attention, for**

> their wingbeats are barely audible. Loud
> breathing is enough to drown them out.
> This is astonishing: my hearing does not
> improve, yet I hear them better and better. I
> must have butterfly hearing.

This is a story about resiliency. And ultimately, about love. Love of life. I heard Alan Jones say that "indiscriminate and unconditional love *may* be at the heart of reality, but that's too vague a thing to bet your life on." I get the point. This all sounds good on paper, but it is not an easy sell, especially when we live in a world where we can put money down on the promised land of resolution—which is any fantasy place we can go (physically or mentally) to consume fictitious resolve. We live in a world where we are fueled by the promises of that imaginary day when all will be easier. Are we there yet?

Resilience is what happens when we give up control and are willing to embrace the ambiguity. And in that ambiguity, to hear the wingbeats of butterflies.

Are we there yet?

We live like four-year-old children. Five minutes out of the driveway on any family trip we ask, "Are we there yet?" We speak of life—our relationships, our job, our calling—in terms of what remains to be done, playing and replaying the sentences in our minds, all of which begin with "if only."

It is no wonder. Our western mindset seeks western solutions: WWTD? (What would technology do?) Now, for fast relief from schedules out of control, life out of balance, we offer more organized palm pilots. You've got to be impressed with the genius here. What a great cultural paradigm: Do you have a problem?

Here's the solution: We give you something to buy. We simplify your life by adding more to it.

Toward what end? We are promised closure. Control. Destination. Even tidiness.

We say we want a balanced life, but there is a difference between being balanced and being organized. This is not just about reallocating time. At some point we learn that life cannot be managed as if it were pneumonia or some treatable disease. As long as life is about tomorrow—or eternity—we cannot rest until we arrive. But what if we are not going anywhere? What if we are simply living? What if we are—today—already on sacred ground?

The implication is that we live our life as a journey and not as a destination, bent on arrival, damning the minutes as we pace the aisles waiting for the haven of accomplishment or completion. With the sacred necessity of resilience, our focus changes. And quite literally, by serendipity, we live in the moment.

Regardless of our circumstances, life pulls us inexorably toward love and beauty, even though it may be wrapped in aching pain or delicious hope. To engage this pull, this fuel that feeds life, is the sacred necessity of resilience. Which means that resilience allows us to live with intention. Now. We do not put off until tomorrow what can be embraced, enjoyed, felt, or experienced today. This includes our sadness, pain, and grief.

Where does one get resilience? Or butterfly hearing?

Is this a gene given to the lucky?

Or a product of willpower bestowed on those who work harder?

Learning the daffodil principle

I am a sucker for any story about flowers, so a friend sent me this story about daffodils. It is told by a southern California grandmother who learned the sacred necessity of resilience in an unusual garden:

Several times my daughter Carolyn had telephoned to say, "Mother, you must come see the daffodils before they are over." I wanted to go, but it was a two-hour drive from Laguna to Lake Arrowhead. "I will come next Tuesday," I promised, a little reluctantly, on her third call.

Next Tuesday dawned cold and rainy. Still, I had promised. When I walked into Carolyn's house, hugged and greeted my grandchildren, I said, "Forget the daffodils. The road is invisible in the fog, and there is nothing in the world except you and these children that I want to see bad enough to drive another inch."

Carolyn smiled calmly, "We drive in this all the time, Mother,"

"Well, you won't get me back on the road until it clears, and then I'm heading for home."

"Okay. But I was hoping you'd take me over to the garage to pick up my car."

"How far is that?"

"Just a few blocks. And I'll drive."

After several minutes, I had to ask, "Where are we going? This isn't the way to the garage."

"We're going the long way," Carolyn smiled. "By way of the daffodils."

"Carolyn," I said sternly, "please turn around."

"It's all right, Mother, I promise. And you'll never forgive yourself if you miss this experience."

After another twenty minutes, we turned onto a small gravel road. Off to the side stood a small church. On the far side of the church I saw a hand-lettered sign, "Daffodil Garden." We got out of the car; each took a child's hand and began walking down a pathway.

As we turned a corner on the path, I looked up and gasped. Before me lay the most glorious sight. It looked as though someone had taken a great vat of golf balls and poured it down over the mountain peak and slopes. The flowers were planted in majestic, swirling patterns—great ribbons and swaths of deep orange, white, lemon yellow, salmon pink, saffron, and butter yellow. Each different colored variety was planted as a group so that it swirled and flowered like its own river with its own unique hue. There were five acres of flowers.

"Who has done this?" I asked.

"The woman who lives here on this property. That's her house." Carolyn pointed to a well kept A-frame house that looked small and modest in the midst of this entire splendor.

We walked up to the house. On the patio a poster was tacked to the front post. "Answers to the questions I know you are asking," it said.

Number one—50,000 bulbs.

Number two—one at a time by one woman with two hands, two feet and a very little brain.

Number three—began in 1958.

There it was, the daffodil principle. For me, that story was life changing. I thought of this woman whom I had never met, who, more than forty years before, had begun, one bulb at a time, to bring her vision of beauty and joy to an obscure mountaintop. Planting one bulb at a time, year after year, had changed her world. My world.

This unknown woman had forever changed the world in which she lived. She created something magnificent. Something of ineffable and indescribable beauty and inspiration. The principle her daffodil garden taught me is one of the greatest principles of celebration. Learning to move toward our goals and desires one step at a time, and learning to love the doing, learning to use the accumulation of time. When we multiply tiny pieces of time with small increments of daily effort, we too will find that we can accomplish magnificent things. An ordinary woman creates something of beauty and inspiration by practicing the sacred necessity of resilience.

With the sacred necessity of resilience we are not swayed by immediate gratification or public accolades.

Life is an aerobic sport

There is something quite cathartic in reducing life to a bumper sticker. So here's my contribution: Life is an aerobic sport.

You remember aerobics? That series of exercises designed to raise the heartbeat to a certain level (a level I'm convinced is humanly impossible). It is an activity which requires twenty or thirty minutes of sustained exercise. And it is an activity which must be practiced at least three days a week to be any benefit to the cardiovascular system.

But there's more. Aerobics, by its very definition, goes on forever. I cannot say, "I did aerobics last week." No, I simply took an aerobic class. It is the same with the word diet. I cannot say, "I dieted today." No, I just postponed lunch until tomorrow. I can, however, say, "I am dieting." Because, like aerobics, it is a lifestyle.

Do you remember the first time you tried an aerobic class? I thought, "This will be no problem." Within ten minutes after the workout had begun, I thought, "I think I'm going to die now." Both of my lungs had collapsed, and my legs stopped functioning. But I did not quit. I didn't want to look like a lightweight. Instead I shouted a prayer. The music in the gymnasium was so loud no one heard me. It was a short prayer, "God, I don't want to die here."

I need to explain. This was several years ago. Remember when spandex was first introduced? I had just bought a brand new blue spandex aerobic outfit. Here's my theory: you don't want to die looking like that.

I need to give you some insight into my dysfunction. After the aerobic class, did I spend twenty minutes cooling down? No. I proceeded immediately to the weight room. Why? Because I paid a lot of money for this club and I wanted to get physically fit today. Even if it killed me.

In the weight room a young man, muscular, self-assured, some poster child for steroids, asked me if I wanted to be on a weight program. I didn't realize I could say no.

So I nodded, and said, "Sure."

"Great," he sounded enthused, picked up a clipboard with a file and asked, "Now, what do you want to accomplish with your weight program?"

Again, I did not know the alternatives. So I told him, "I want to build bulk."

He looked at me, and suggested, "You mean move bulk, don't you?"

He directed me to the bench press. You lay on your back and push weight up off your chest. The weights were already on the machine, so you simply place a pin in the weight you choose. In my oxygen deprived stupor I tried 80 pounds.

I could not lift 80 pounds.

My instructor wrote on his clipboard, "Bench press. 35 pounds."

Another young man, shorter than me, put the pin at 200 pounds and executed twenty repetitions. I felt my self-esteem leave me, like a helium balloon with a leak.

My instructor began to laugh. Soon he was hitting his knee with his clipboard. "You're new here, aren't you?"

"How did you guess?"

"Well, for one thing, you have on this new blue aerobic outfit. The guys in the weight room voted, and they think you're a doll."

He goes on, "And for another, all you new guys are the same. You all think you're going to look like Arnold Schwarzenegger overnight. See that guy (pointing to the shorter man bench-pressing 200 pounds)? He's been lifting weights for ten years, four days a week. You've been lifting weights for five minutes. Let that be a lesson to you."

It was. I never went back.

To give him credit, he was right. Life is not somewhere you arrive, life is the direction you are going. Life is not a destination. Life is the journey.

If we see life as a destination, we're asking the wrong questions. We ask "how" questions: "How successful am I?" "How together am I?" "How settled am I?" "How muscular am I?" "How spiritual am I?"

"How" asks for some external measurement. Am I accomplished? Is my life under control? Is my desk clean?

The answers are always measured by comparison. Answering a "how" question is like putting on a show. You know, posturing and preening. Yes, I think I'm accomplished, but is it enough? We become like an anorexic losing weight. There is never enough weight to lose.

And now we're at the mercy of "what will they think?" We find ourselves living by sheer willpower, compulsion, obligation, duress, and constraint—as if we could force a resilient life. "I want to live my life like the daffodil woman. So tell me how. *Now*. And I will work to achieve it. I will make it happen." In the end, it is no different than straining to force happiness. We sound like parents at Disneyland.

"We're here at Disneyland, you better start having a good time!"

"You better change your attitude. Do you know how much your parents spent on this trip?"

My favorite was overhearing a mother tell her three children, "Shut up and smile!"

We could do the same thing here. I could make it my duty to make you feel guilty about not having a resilient life. But that's not loving life, that's coercion. Or compulsion. As if it is a requirement to be resilient.

To exacerbate our dilemma, at some point my childhood guilt kicks in, bemoaning all the time I have wasted, if only I had begun to practice this principle forty-five years ago.

With compulsion, we feel the need to justify our time, our balanced life, our schedules. It is like grownup show-and-tell. The goal is the same: impressing people.

"I used to struggle, but not any more," one man told me at a recent seminar, wearing that frozen grin.

"Oh really," I answered, "when did you quit struggling?"

"About an hour ago."

It's clear to me that we need new questions to change our focus from a destination mentality to a journey mentality.

In what ways do I treat my days, my relationships, as a journey and not as a destination?

In what ways am I living a rounded, whole life with integrity?

In what ways is my life infused with passion, purpose, heart, and grace?

These questions allow us to celebrate small victories and little gifts. When my attention is monopolized by the future, some yet to be determined time of arrival, I fail to see the gentle doses of grace that fill my days.

Which means, I'm not going to tell you to be resilient. I'm going to tell you to live with passion, purpose, heart, and grace. Which is another way of saying that each of these sacred necessities is about spillage. They are the result of living with passion, purpose, heart, and grace. You can't force them. Or coerce them.

The aerobic principle answers the question about the fuel of resilience. With it I make a conscious distinction between journey and destination. Resilience as destination requires willpower to the tenth power. I may just as well have my brow surgically furrowed. I grit and concentrate, all the while envious of those with superior mental strength. And in the arena of faith, the stakes seem higher.

Try harder, I am told. Try harder, I tell myself. Try harder, I tell others, hoping to spread the inconvenience.

Suit yourself. I'm going to eat a pint of Häagen-Dazs.

It is not where we arrive, it is the direction we are going

A group of us are putting together a book on the natural history of the island on which we live. It is a sense of place piece, about the island's critters and quirky plants and leftover volcanic soil and old growth cedar trees and salmon streams and heron rookery. It's about why we live here and why we are so smitten by it all.

Pat—a fellow writer—and I had the task of taking the thirty or so manuscripts and setting them in some sort of readable and coherent progression. I went to her place for an afternoon of work. She lives on the east side of the island, and her house—the original portion built in the 1930s—sits on two acres of low bank waterfront, looking out over the Puget Sound toward Seattle and the Cascade mountain range. We sat, working at a desk facing the water. The water lay relatively still, with cormorants hanging out on makeshift moorings, like bored teenagers without a car.

Pat and I talked about the chapters and about the book. We talked about the water and the orca whales, now congregated around our island for their annual salmon feeding. And Pat asked about my father. She knew he had cancer and was currently in the middle of his chemo treatments. Pat also wears a turban, the obligatory concession to an alliance with the powerful drugs waging war on her behalf in her own body.

I told her that my father was in good spirits, knowing that his cancer was at stage one, and that there was a reasonable shot at containing it.

I asked her about her health, but was reluctant to press.

"I'm at stage four," she told me matter-of-factly. "That's all there is. There are no more stages."

From the visits with my father's oncologist, I knew that stage four cancer is aggressive, meaning that the disease has spread throughout the body, possibly into the lungs or the bone marrow. It means that the best medicine can do is maintain the status quo. Stage four is when doctors begin to talk about time. When they reluctantly tell you how long you have to live.

"Is it in your lungs?" I asked.

"They've seen some spots on the x-rays, but don't know what to make of them yet." She paused and we watched a cormorant cruise a few inches above the water, as if the water and bird were negative magnets, keeping an exact spacing between the two. A massive freighter drifted by, a condominium of railway containers, its idle pace certainly belying its mission.

Pat went on, "My oncologist originally told me I'd be on the chemo treatments for nine months. Well, it's been nine months. So I asked her about it. I mean what would happen if we saw that all my blood work hadn't shown any signs of weakening. She told me, 'Then we'll just keep at it.' Which means, of course, that I'll be on chemo forever."

There's just no way to make such a statement and sound unaffected. Or no way to hear it, and go about your day as if the scales of our faith have not been tipped. I listened. Thinking about my father and how when we go into a restaurant together in the small town where he lives he can point to others who have or have had cancer. It's a fraternity I am not privy to. And I can tell it means something to him to know he's not alone in all of this.

As she continued, her eyes clouded. "I wanted my doctor to tell me that she had great news. I wanted her to tell me that I was the lucky one in 500,000 people who beat this thing."

We sat silently. I didn't know what to say after that. Maybe I couldn't handle the obvious. It's true that the temptation to be a constrained cheerleader is visceral. As if there is a need to say something upbeat, to say anything for fear of what the silence may mean. As if silence, left to hang above us, will descend and choke us in its thick sorrow. As if through words we could make something of the moment.

"Are you troubled by any of the other side affects?" I finally asked her.

"No," she smiled. "I'm fortunate there. No nausea. And I still have quite a bit of energy."

I didn't want to ask what that felt like. Knowing that your days are numbered. So we chatted a bit longer. Mostly about the book. It was pleasant, and the truth is that I could have stayed another half hour or so, had a cup of tea, and watched the ships float by. But I didn't want to intrude on her time. That's what I told myself anyway. Or maybe I couldn't handle the obvious. When we live smack-dab in the present it is not easy to suspend our regrets over yesterday or our fears about tomorrow, especially when tomorrow may never come.

At any rate, I had a long list of things to do before the afternoon was up, and my mind started sifting through the pile. You don't want to ignore the list, what with its relentless harangue. So I said my goodbyes and took my leave. We'll see each other again at another of our island writers' get-togethers.

Of course we will.

Resilience involves inviting life—all of life—in

Resilience involves inviting all of life in: the longing, hunger, wildness, energy, appetite, hope, humor, beauty, and irony. We are not outrunning life. Or outrunning the bad parts of life. Only when we embrace do we see.

I see now that with my friend Pat, I was afraid to honor that space, waiting instead for some issue to be resolved, for miracles to spirit us past the messiness. I wanted to see beyond the mess. I know now that such a thing is possible only if I embrace the mess, this clay of life.

If I run, I do not honor.

If I do not honor, I do not allow for the space that enables me to give, receive, move, or grow.

There is a Taoist saying of Chuang Tzu: "One has to be in the same place every day, watch the dawn from the same house, hear the same birds awake each morning, to realize how inexhaustibly rich and different is sameness."

There is something liberating in the notion of life as a journey. We are no longer encumbered by the need—the compulsion—to arrive. Today can be sacred ground indeed.

There is a poignant story about a British politician who died some years ago. His memoirs were published posthumously. They included political writings and personal journal entries. Included was this cryptic entry: "I had to take my son fishing today. I didn't want to go. It was cold and damp. I was tired and in a foul mood. There was much to do, and time was wasting. I doubt that we caught any fish. I was glad we never had to do that again."

The son, now an adult, read his father's memoir, and seeing the date and entry, it triggered a memory. He retrieved a journal that he had kept as a child. He found the date and read, "Had the greatest day of my life today. I went fishing with my dad."

Watering the resilience

When we would walk our dogs each morning we would take the same route. Down our gravel driveway, through the canyon, up a steep incline to the main road, where we walked the shoulder one additional mile before turning back. It was the same route every day. Two miles.

And for me, it was the same walk every day. Literally. But for my dogs, the walk was never the same.

As the walk begins, my mind is already racing with the affairs of the day, and I quicken my pace in order to finish the obligation. My dogs seem oblivious to worry. They are eager to explore, to discover, to happen upon some game or activity which requires their full resolve. They need to alternate between peeing and smelling, a dog's variation of email, checking to see who in the neighborhood left a message. On this particular morning the air is crisp, the temperature just above freezing. The grass on either side of the road is marked, some elaborate map, with footprints. I stop, briefly, to watch both dogs in a frenzy to find the buried treasure—a rabbit, or pheasant, or raccoon. Journey indeed.

It's time for me to practice—affirm—what I believe. For practical reasons we (my wife, son, and I) must move from the house that we love.

I know intellectually that living is a form of not being sure. Even so, it's the limbo that gets you. And for all my preaching to the contrary, I can't wait until we get to some resolution. Where will we live?

I once read, "The trip becomes a journey after you've lost your luggage." Was it on a coffee mug at a souvenir shop, next to the flamingo lamps?

It is a late autumn misting-shower, a stubborn and emphatic drizzle, as if the sky is gray cheesecloth doing its best to keep the water at bay. The view out my window is dramatically different from any of the days over the past month or so, now with a deep blue-gray lens on the camera, as if made intentionally gloomy for some movie scene. The backdrop of trees is perceptibly closer, and the garden area feels smaller and deserted.

I spent time yesterday out in the garden. On the one hand, I felt terribly frustrated with our house-sale-limbo, and its emotional strictures. Our house has been on the market now for a bit over two months (of itself, hardly worrisome, but unsettling as the predetermined time frame is ignored). Are we there yet?

Each extra day now feels burdensome, and the extra time spent waiting feels wasted. There is so much, after all, that begs to be done. So I say my goodbyes with a cool and critical eye, noticing every defect and imperfection, in part angry that I haven't had the opportunity or foresight to correct them, in part wanting a clean slate. On the other hand, still enamored with the garden's charm, noticing a pocket of bloom and foliage in the long border (for all intents and purposes left to its own devises since late July save a little water now and again) with rudbeckia (Black-eyed Susan), filigreed bronze fennel, and lamb's-wool-soft, common sage, all back-dropped by the massive sericea rose. It is a carefree and blissful scene, and I am happy in spite of myself.

Now the empty bench looks lonely in the winter light, flanked by a hydrangea, its rickety and twisted canes bowed under the weight of dried pom-poms, as if a scene petrified in time. Underneath, egg-yolk-yellow primroses ignore the conditions, and persist in bloom.

The upper bed, buoyed by interludes of winter sun, gives an impression of perkiness. Miscanthus grass stands as an upright bronze geyser. The lower bed, screened by fir and hemlock, is relegated to winter shade that gives it an abandoned and hopeless air. The deck in our lower garden, our summer roost, becomes a wintertime holding area for gallon pots—cuttings and division for next year, or gifts for friends.

I decide to walk around the garden to see if there is anything I can do to tidy up. The air is brisk and refreshing. I get sidetracked from my original plans and find myself hunched near the ground, examining the furry nubbed shoots of catmint, marveling at the pluck and tenacity of such tender sprouts. And I remember that garden novice hunting for his dahlia shoots. I smile, feel my heart begin to flutter, and I realize that it's going to be a great day after all.

friendship

"If the body is in pain, one of the first things to look for is infection; if the soul is in pain, we might look for lack of friendship."

—Thomas Moore

7

My putt, seven feet straight up hill, comes up short. "I can't believe I didn't hit that," I fume, feeling the anguish endemic to golf addiction.

Roy seems oblivious to my melodrama, happily three-putting on every green. It is enviable, this lack of talent.

We're in Stanley Park, an evergreen peninsula at the west end of Vancouver, British Columbia. Stanley Park is what every city needs. An elegant, civil, open public space filled with cedar, hemlock, fir, maple, and chestnut trees.

This is an idyllic day. Temperature in the mid-70s, the park alive with movement. Groups of school children saunter and chatter, surrounded by chaperones keeping the herd in formation. Men and women, dressed in all whites, lawn bowling, give an air of old world civility. Bicyclers and skateboarders forge a stream of motion, on the grass areas there are people strolling or ambling (one is never sure), while others—oblivious to public opinion—snuggle and whisper.

Stumps from old growth cedar and redwood trees establish an impressive presence, representing noble and majestic trees that lived five hundred years ago. Out of the stumps—as if the stumps are giant wooden pots—grow mature trees: mimosa, cedar, and cypress. The stumps bear the tell-tale scars from the buckboard, where turn-of-the-century loggers notched holes to place a plank on which two men could stand and saw.

We are playing the Stanley Park pitch-and-putt golf course. On the hole ahead of us there is a young couple. She is earnest and eager. He is teaching her, a steady stream of advice and direction, his tone on edge. "No, you want to swing all the way back. Like this." As in other publicly embarrassing occasions, you feel compelled to look away. And yet you want to intervene. But you have to let them learn it on their own. The young woman swings and misses the ball completely. I look away.

"We're here to work on this book on friendship," Roy reminds me.

"Ah, yes."

"You realize it was two years ago I suggested this project," He makes the announcement casually, but pleased with himself, as if there are points scored.

"Really, two years?" My mind focused on the next shot.

"Two years," he says again. "Can you believe that? And what have we accomplished, not a damn thing."

"You mean like getting your son through high school? Keeping our marriages together? And finding meaning in our jobs?" I try to sound facetious.

"Well. We've stayed friends. These days, maybe that's enough."

So, are we friends?

In the movie *Tombstone*, Doc Holiday is asked why he is willing to risk his life in a fight he could easily avoid. "Because," he replied, "Wyatt Earp is my friend."

"Well I got a lot of friends," the man said, incredulous.

"I don't," Doc Holiday answered.

Which means that if you are lucky enough to have a good friend, it wouldn't hurt to pay attention. And ask the crucial questions:

In today's world, what does it mean to be a friend? And what does it takes to nurture that friendship?

The last thing I want is to get mired in the definition business. Except to say this: You can go through your whole life, and in the end count your close friends on one hand, and in so doing, consider yourself wonderfully blessed.

'Friend' is one of those words—like love or dysfunction—that has suffered from overkill. In our western culture where everyone is our friend, we have rendered the word bloodless. (As a result, in North America, it's popular to have everyone be our friend. But to paraphrase Soren Kierkegaard, "If everyone is our friend, then no one is our friend." If we are intimate with everyone, we are intimate with no one.)

We have enough expressions and euphemisms for friendship to make the head spin. Some folks have an address book or BlackBerry chock-full of friends, enough to fill the Queen Mary for cocktails, so go figure. Yet deep down we know that there are friends, and there are *friends*.

We live in a world where we have friends, "just friends," playmates, good friends, real good friends (wink, wink), co-workers, team members, instant message buddies, best friends, soul mates, and then people we date, who somehow are none of the above. Except if the dating ends on an unfortunate note, then they become "still friends." Or "we get along real good." Or, with great irony, the word friend can become a euphemism for "get lost." "I told him I wanted to be nothing more than friends," her voice said, while her body language was loud and clear, "What a jackass!"

It's not too difficult to see that our overburdened expectations of romance have pushed friendship to the periphery of our lives. Romance is the "holy grail" of our culture, promising happiness, freedom from gray skies, and completion.

Dining in a restaurant, alone, after I had finished a speaking engagement, I discovered this holy grail. (Parenthetically, let me say that I enjoy eating alone, much to the mortification of the hostess, who gives me the look reserved for lonely middle-aged men. I ignore it, or pretend I'm on a weekend pass from an institution.) The waitress asked about my meal, and then, "So, do you live here?"

"No. I'm from Seattle."

"What were you doing here."

"A seminar. On relationships."

"Oh."

Later, returning to the table, she asked, "Can I ask you a question?"

160

"Of course."

"Are you in a relationship now?"

I couldn't help myself. "Yes," I told her, "several of them."

Her eyes stared, incredulous. "How do you get away with that?"

"None of them know about the others."

She doesn't laugh.

And then she tells me, "Well unfortunately, I'm not in a relationship now. I haven't found the right one."

Listen to us. "We haven't found the right one." Merle Shain is right. "We don't know much about friendship really. We think of a friend as someone to spend time with when there isn't anyone else around who really matters. And when we have a vacancy in our life for a lover or a spouse, we look for someone to fill than spot."

We may not know as much as we think we do

I am convinced that people who talk too much about friendship don't experience it. (The same holds true for matters of sex, intimacy, and God.)

I heard someone once say that a North American person visits the Middle East for a week, returns to the United States, and writes a book about the factions in relationships there. Another person visits for a month, returns home, and writes a magazine article. While another lives there for a year. After he returns home, he remains silent.

We may not know as much as we think we do. And that, blessedly, is a good thing. So this should be liberating. We can begin our exploration of friendship with some humility and wonder. We can let go of our need to have the answers provided by the correct script, as if a script guarantees success.

One is rightfully suspicious of those who talk too much about friendship, because those who understand these subjects never say much about them. As Eugene Kennedy says in his book *On Being a Friend*, their "silence is the symbol of the security that is the seal of mature friendship."

Why? The reality is simple (books and seminars not withstanding). No one knows, really, how to make friends, or how we should die, or what it is that will make us wiser about the losses and griefs of either experience.

Here's the good news. Once we let go of the need for answers, we can receive a gift. Or, in the words of Thomas Moore,

> **Friendship is not essentially a union
> of personalities, it is an attraction and
> magnetism of souls . . . The fact that it's
> impossible to explain just what makes
> someone a great friend, or that we can't
> go out and apply a formula for finding
> true friends, indicates how deep and
> unintentional friendship can be. It is as
> though souls recognize the hidden treasure
> in each other and forge the alliance,
> while the conscious mind goes on with its
> intentions, hopes, and expectations.**

Friendship begins when we take a chance

I want to commit to friendships. So I write this out of selfishness. As a reminder to myself that friendship is a non-negotiable. In truth, I am still enamored by self-sufficiency, accomplishments, reputation, and stuff. But deep down, I know that life can be lived without all of these things. But I can't be fully human or fully alive without friends. I find it interesting that Jesus kept pointing this out to his disciples. He cautioned them from rejoicing in their resumes. And he invited them to be his friends. He didn't tell them what to believe. He invited them into a relationship.

This much I know for certain. Friendship is not acquired. It is made. It is a river that runs through our days. With choices weathered, rounded, seasoned, and fashioned in that river that runs through time and experience. Friendship is a process of movement. Creating and co-creating. Molding and being molded. And a friendship can only stay alive if it is intentional.

I could argue the case I suppose. I could quote St. Francis of de Sales, who spoke of friendship as *"necessitudo"*—necessary. Or quote Cicero, who stated "friendship is the sun of life . . . the best gift which the immortal gods have given us with the exception of wisdom." Or, I could use modern studies which show that "people with good friends usually have less stress and may even live longer." The *Seattle Times* reported that in a study of 22,800 men and women over sixty-five, "those with more friends had a lower risk of health problems and recovered faster when they did develop them."

Or, I could choose to commit. It's really as simple as that. We put ourselves on the line. We are intentional. We say, "This is important to me." There's the caveat. Friendship requires something on my part because friendship is a declaration, and no friendship happens by default.

It is of little consequence how the relationship turns out. What is vital is my intentional decision at this moment. "I am the sum of my commitments," wrote Martin Buber, "or, in other words, I am what I chose to stand up and be counted for, and those choices define me."

It means that I choose to communicate. To ask. Tell. Play. Invite. Be present. Push. Give and take. Be a sounding board. Write a note.

The alternative? Merle Shain is right again:

> **All those people who don't commit, all those people who are acting like they are not really on this trip, and all those people who have put themselves on hold, they are cheating themselves, and in seeking to have wings, they've forgotten that they need roots as well.**

"It doesn't matter how well you know yourself. What matters is how you relate to what you do know."

—Buddha

"So. Why are we friends?" my friend asked.

We were spending the afternoon drinking coffee. Talking. Laughing. Theorizing. And reminiscing. Interrupted by an hour or so wandering the stacks of a nearby bookstore, where the only books on friendship were for or by women. We asked for a book of friendship for or by men. We were told by a cheerful associate that there was one, and we found ourselves staring at a shelf with books about war. And women wonder why we are so angry?

In the end, we knew what we needed to do. To reaffirm the choices we made so long ago. Even more importantly, to create a liturgy of friendship. And to find out what these lessons could teach us and others who may be asking the same questions:

What keeps me from being a friend? What is it that makes me enjoy his or her company one day, and push him or her away the next? Why is it that I find pleasure in the ebb and flow of one day, and seeds of resentment buried in the next?

What are the ways we can celebrate this friendship? We are asked to define our lives by our vocations, or possessions, or accomplishments. But never by our friendships. Well, we've got it backwards. It's the friends who surround, encircle, and embrace us that tell us who we are.

What allows me to be a better friend? What will it take for me to pay attention, to listen, to be intentional?

Friendship is a gift—a mixture of mystery, grace, and death (or loss)

I don't want to pretend that friendship is easy—or that it doesn't exact a price. There are plenty of reasons not to be friends. Maybe you can relate to this poem:

> **Will you be my friend?**
> **There are so many reasons why you never**
> **should**
> **I'm seldom predictably the same,**
> **I bluster and I brag,**
> **I seek attention like a child,**
> **I brood and I pout,**
> **my anger can be wild**
> **but underneath I shake a little every day**
> **more than strangers would ever know.**
> **And I wonder—**
> **if I show you my trembling side,**
> **will you still be my friend?**

We've all been used by people feigning friendship. We've all given more than our share. And we've all held back our cards, and played them very close to our chest. We've been embarrassed by foolish choices. We've seen friendship and romance become commingled and too complicated. And we've invested in friendship, only to have our friend move away.

Friends, after all, do hurt each other. It comes with the territory. Ties can be most precarious. And some friendships, it seems, are temporary. They offer support during some important interval in our life and inexplicably vanish.

Every healthy relationship includes pain and grief. There is no shortcut. Pain from loss is inevitable. These small deaths are woven into the friendship tapestry. The loss of naivete, the breech of trust, the loss of an unblemished picture of life, the loss of our heart, the loss of idealism, the loss of unrealistic expectations, the loss by death, or geographic displacement, or shift in responsibilities.

Grief is inevitable because every relationship is, at best, an imperfect connection. We must all navigate among the fault lines.

The point is that friendship is not the absence of our problems, it is our problems. How do we come to embrace the loss that comes with being connected? How do we recognize that the gift and the risk are intermingled?

My cell phone rings. There is a cacophony of noise. A wrong number no doubt. But I have nothing pressing, no social agenda waiting, so I decide to listen to sort out the mystery. The noise abates and I hear music, a song I quickly recognize.

Billy Joel's "Piano Man." But the voice is not Joel's, though equally recognizable. It is Elton John's. After the song, the crowd erupts. The next song is one of Elton's, this time sung by Billy Joel. During the next salvo of applause and squall, I hear my friend's voice shouting into a cupped hand, "Hey, buddy. I had tickets near the front row. I knew you couldn't be here but know these are two of your favorites, so I wanted you to hear a little bit of the magic. I'm glad you're my friend."

> **Here is the place I belong,**
> **a place where I am wanted, apprehended,**
> **and unique.**
> **Friendship begins when we honor each**
> **other.**

Honor by self-care and self-nurture

Granted, this is an odd place to begin. Yet, without ongoing self-care, I enter too many relational encounters with a ravenous hole in my soul, and I am destined to be disappointed, even resentful.

Self-care or self-nurture is another way of saying that we are doing the work that will give us the foundation we need to maintain emotional integrity for the other tough work of friendship—communication, conflict resolution, compromise, fault-line repair.

Self-care and self-nurture are costly because they require taking responsibility, self-acceptance, giving up being a victim.

"Friendship literally catches us off guard—when we are not preening ourselves to make an impression or protecting ourselves from the possibility of truly meeting someone else."

What did I do this week that was nurturing for me?

Honor the inner life of the other

"Real friends hold open house in their psyches for each other," Eugene Kennedy writes, "they can wander about, picking up now this and now that, familiarizing themselves with the territory like unsighted persons sensitively establishing a map of a room."

This is only possible if I have given up any sense of ownership or possessiveness. Friendship is primarily set apart by this "otherness." Respect for separateness is what distinguishes friends from lovers.

Honor as a place of restoration in a stormy world

Real friends are those who, when you've made a fool of yourself, don't feel you've done a permanent job.

They provide us with a shelter where we don't have to do battle. (The irony, of course, is that in our woundedness we project our insecurity and pain on to those we love the most.)

Real friends create a sanctuary where confidentiality is honored. In the practice of friendship, we might keep this important aspect of our soul in mind: its need for containment, held by and acknowledged in gentleness and kindness.

Rabbi Harold Kushner tells this story about friendship:

> I was sitting on a beach one summer day,
> watching two children, a boy and a girl,
> playing in the sand. They were hard at
> work building an elaborate sand castle by
> the waters edge, with gates and towers and
> moats and internal passages. Just when they
> had nearly finished their project, a big wave
> came along and knocked it down, reducing
> it to a heap of wet sand. I expected the
> children to burst into tears, devastated by
> what had happened to all their hard work.
> But they surprised me. Instead, they ran up
> the shore away from the water, laughing
> and holding hands, and sat down to build
> another castle. I realize that they had taught
> me an important lesson. All the things in
> our lives, all the complicated structures we
> spend so much time and energy creating,
> are built on sand. Only our relationships
> to other people endure. Sooner or later, the
> wave will come along and knock down
> what we have worked so hard to build up.
> When that happens, only the person who

had somebody's hand to hold will be able to laugh.

Honor in rituals and sacred spaces

We're sitting around the pool at a rental house in Palm Springs, California. The sun is low in the afternoon sky, behind the mountains—a spellbinding backdrop with the treeless mountains a nearly bruised purple in this late afternoon light.

The reason for this gathering? My fiftieth birthday. I look around at the faces of the friends who have given a weekend to be a part of this festivity. Men are sitting, lounging, smiling, listening to music (great music from the 60s), swimming, talking, pontificating, reading, baiting, taunting, ignoring, testosterone strutting, confiding, recollecting, and laughing from the belly.

We talk about politics, midlife, our children (for some, grandchildren), memories, sex (stories both factual and wistful). For three days we have told stories (the facts sometimes in dispute, but every story still true and evocative), argued theology (the linear black and white thinking of our youth giving way to an embrace of ambiguity and the unceasing requirement of grace), commiserated about life's injustices (both perceived and real, although mostly perceived and often exaggerated), celebrated milestones (none having to do with personal achievements, as there is little room here to hang your ego on what you've done, or failed to do). I saw a sign once, "No cute persona wanted here; only the real stuff."

This is the real stuff.

We are blessed friends.

And it doesn't get any better than this.

In friendship there may be more not-doing than doing. Friendship doesn't ask for a great deal of activity, but it does require loyalty and presence.

I've know these men for over twenty years. The realization settles. Individual histories scroll by my mind's eye. The histories not all without difficulty. In some relationships, years of distance, hard feelings, unmet expectations. Followed by conversation, reconnecting, and reconciliation. And all of it bringing us here to this place. On this afternoon, when the sound of laughter saturates and charges the air with the fullness of life, I think of Frederick Buechner's great observation: "Friends are people you make a part of your life just because you feel like it. Basically your friends are not your friends for any particular reason. They are your friends for no particular reason."

That makes sense to me. There's no balance sheet at work here. This is no working group from which to glean insights, no "five easy steps" on how to make friendship sell. We are an amalgamation, a tapestry of all those who have shared in our lives. One thing is certain: The few people who have truly passed through us and us through them, until the dreams, images, memories are past sorting out, these people become precious links to our continuity . . . If we try to bury the images of others who meant so much, part of us dies with them. How much greater our aliveness if we can come to a freestanding friendship with those who have shared us.

I once wrote to a friend, "I was thinking about your comments—re: being excessively fragile and vulnerable—thinking that I didn't know what to say, sipping my Graham's Six Grapes Port while watching the Sonics get their rear ends kicked by Denver, and remembering the times in my life when I felt on the edge or in some way susceptible to shattering (both shattered, and shattering someone, anyone around me), and trying to remember what triggered those times, and I came up with zero. If all else fails, I'd be more than happy to pour you a glass of Port and offer you a chair on the back deck to watch the sun set over Puget Sound, and hope for a little luck that maybe we'd see a bald eagle float by, and tell you that I don't know much, but 'that sure is a damn fine eagle, isn't it?' Who knows, before the light gives way completely, we could wander over to the garden and take a hit of fragrance from the rose *Souvenir de la Malmasion*, and marvel at the different ways the gods let us get intoxicated, loitering in the moment, knowing full well that this drunkenness—like any other—comes with a price; the bittersweet reality that it can never quite fill that pit in our soul, even though it comes close. Or, we can stay put on the deck, crank up the music, let Mr. Clapton fill the dark and the empty spaces, swap stories with a good friend, and hope that the gods are taking notes on recommendations for ways to make eternity tolerable."

So there's no magic here. No self-help or easy steps. But we've all been there, and can make a strong case for the necessity of friendships that last, and make a difference.

Honor as a way of helping one another "taste life"

Call it the "Thelma and Louise factor." Friends pump life into each other.

K. C. Jones is a respected name in basketball. In the eighties, he led the Boston Celtics to two NBA championships. And in 1988 he retired. Boston honored him with a comfortable front-office job with a generous salary. For all intents and purposes, he could coast.

But he chose not to. In 1989, K. C. Jones moved to Seattle to become an assistant coach for the Seattle Supersonics under Bernie Bickerstaff.

And people in Boston didn't understand. Why would a legend leave a cushy job to be, of all things, an assistant coach?

At age fifty-seven.

In Seattle.

With a man who was his assistant sixteen years before.

"Pure and simple, it's Bernie," says Jones. "When he said, 'Kase, would you be interested in coming on out to work?' I said, 'Wow, that sounds beautiful!' Most people can count their close friends on one hand. Maybe it's one, or two, or five. But close friends you can count on, and Bernie and me count on each other."

The presence of a friend makes a difference

There are friends-of-the-road—people who pass through—and there are friends of the heart. Or this, from Rocky Dennis, the main character in the movie *Mask* (about a teenager with a congenital disfiguring bone disorder), "Eric's my friend at school. Ben's my friend for life." The presence of a friend makes a difference.

The evening desert air is cooler. I am still cavorting with my friends in Palm Springs. As the stillness from the evening air settles, its weight seems to slow the earth's tempo. My mind replays the day, gratefully letting go of any need to measure. I hear the background music, and Leonard Cohen's grave voice is a fitting benediction, "There is a crack in everything. That's how the light shines in. That's how the light shines in."

And I think about this book. It has been percolating for a few years. When I began, I collected notes, quotes, stories, observations, and erudite bumper stickers. I set my sights high, you know, insights that would enable people to live life fully engaged. My collection filled three manilla folders. In the beginning, I wanted clarity of insight, that kind of propositional certainty hawked by books and speakers *ad nauseam*. Somewhere along the way, I realized that life is not about having correct information. It is not about what I believe. It is about what I commit to.

Thomas Moore keenly observed that "the soul requires many varieties of vessels and many kinds of spaces in order to work day by day with the raw material life serves up. Friendship is one of the most effective and precious of those containers." This raw material—an elixir of hopes, desires, yearnings, aloneness, sadness, grief, and joy—is our thorough, complete, and uncompromising humanness.

No. I don't have a motto or a bumper sticker. But I know, as I sit here among friends under the desert sky, that life is precious, and, at moments like this, unalloyed. Pure. Even white hot. And too easily watered down with analysis.

It is enough to let it settle for a spell. Percolate. Ferment.

If you're lucky you recognize and embrace these moments, especially in the face of a cultural deluge promising another, better life. There is solace in the moments when we have no need to capitulate to such promises. And we rest under the full weight of life, this life.

Natalie Goldberg tells the story about the three months she spent in Jerusalem, and an encounter with her Israeli landlady (a woman in her fifties):

> Her TV set was broken and she called a repairman. It took him four visits to fix the screen.
>
> "But you knew even before he came the first time what was wrong. He could have brought the correct tube and fixed it immediately."
>
> She looked at me in astonishment. "Yes, but then we couldn't have had a relationship, sat and drunk tea and discussed the progress of the repairs."
>
> Of course, the goal is not to fix a machine but to have relationships.

Yes.

"The best beauty product is to have a life. A real life. With challenges, disappointments, stress, and laughter. The much-touted inner beauty is a natural radiance that comes as a result of mental and emotional involvement."

—Veronica Vienne, *The Art of Imperfection*

"I want to know if joy, curiosity, struggle, and compassion bubble up in a person's life. I'm interested in being fully alive."

—Alan Jones

Afterword

The religion of my youth taught me about life after death. I never heard one sermon on life before death. I think about this odd memory on an evening with a full moon above Burton Cove, an inlet on the southern part of our island. The light appears to slither or dance across the water as I drive, listening to Buddy Guy cranked up, and the air cool on my skin. I've spent the day cleaning my garden beds, gathering the debris accumulated from mid-winter weather. Spent stalks. Leaves. I feel the welcome ache of work in every limb my body. The music acts as a salve.

It's not an easy lesson this. Delighting in the smallest things. There are these moments when something akin to contentment overwhelms all desire to alter things.

Which brings to mind one of the great theoretical party questions: If you could turn back the hands of time, and stop it at some particular golden time in your life, and stay there forever, would you? And I remember an afternoon last month, in La Jolla, California, watching my son play his created game of keep-away with the waves that lap on to the beach and scoot forward as if wicked by an enormous paper towel. Zach stays ahead of the advancing water, laughing and cheering. It is the matador and the bull. Parry and thrust. Retreat and

charge. The strictures of time have disappeared for him. He
has only the moment, the game, the wave. A pelican soars
over his head, some great feathered javelin. He points and
laughs and gives me a thumbs up.

I put down my book and write that "we want to bottle what
he has, sell it, and retire wealthy," but recognize that there is
nothing better than contentment and dollops of grace, even
if you are merely the enchanted witness.

I will not tell people I have the answers. . . . It is annoying

When I survey new books about life and the way it should
be lived, I find it wonderfully apropos that there is such a
disagreement on how to be happy. There are books that tell
me I need to act now, waste no time, organize my life, get rid
of slack, and to eliminate wasted space. Another book tells me
that smelling the roses is still the way to go. Or maybe laying
on the back lawn or deck and watching the clouds float by.
One says that the wisdom of the Tao is right for our times,
"Practice not-doing, and everything will fall into place." To
which the other side responds that such wasted time only puts
us further behind and in the end stressed and distracted. And
in my mind I conjure a good old fashioned bar room brawl to
settle this dispute once and for all.

I suppose our temperament determines the way we react to
these commands. In my case, I've tried getting my act together
with a steely and speedy paced performance, and in the end
I agree with Ghandi, "There is more to life than increasing its
speed."

My favorite people are the ones who don't pay attention to the commotion.

Barbara Scott, in her book, *The Stations of Still Creek*, tells this story:

> **Friend dying of cancer says, "Anything extra I've got now is going into riding my motorcycle. Does that make any sense to you?" "Of course. It could be dancing, only I can't dance; turning wood; playing the banjo; riding a motorcycle. Whatever it is when we at last say no one will interrupt me right now and I will not apologize for spending all day on this.**

Places to see before you die

Rummaging in Munro's Bookstore in Victoria, B.C., I saw a great book title, *1000 Places to See Before You Die*. I opened the book at random to "Antibes and the *Hotel de Cap Eden Roc.*" They are right. I have never been there. And, from the pictures, I would love to spend a fortnight or so there.

And I wondered, wouldn't it be something if I turned the pages and found pictures of my wife and son and friends I love? No offense intended to the book. But I miss the point entirely if I fail to see those close to me.

Here on Vashon Island Bob's Bakery is an institution. It is our watering hole. For me, a morning coffee with a pumpkin muffin. This is a sacred ritual.

In front stand two benches, each made of planks of timbers shaved from the side of a tree. They are worn smooth by time. It is the place to sit, sip your coffee, watch the day roll by, and take the island's social pulse.

I sit with Carl Blumgren, one of the long-time islanders. His beard, style, clothing, and weathered look tell you that this day could be unfolding at the turn of the previous century. Carl is a gentle soul, always with a smile and a kind word. "Where's your friend," I ask. (I always see him with Dan Chasen, another long-time islander. I have teased him in the past, telling him that we should just make a bornze statue in front of Bob's and be done with it.) "Oh," he says. "What's today? Tuesday? Well, tomorrow he'll be here about noon. It's our conversation appointment. Every Wednesday."

If you began this book looking for answers, or at the very least recommendations, by this point you've let it go and given yourself over to the day. There are those who find some solace in a good list, to serve as a reminder, and to fuel the undecided parts of our psyche. The least I can do is oblige. So I borrow from a marvelous artist, Mary Anne Radmacher:

Be avid.

Create apart from perfection: risk failure.

Cover your words with sweat.

Excruciatingly touch.

Laugh until you cry.

Dance with your eyes closed.

Understand you die a little everyday.

Be enlivened.

There is no sky here. It is the first thing you notice when you land at SeaTac. There is no sky here. The sky has been replaced with a bulky, stained, gray, dome-shaped tarpaulin.

But then, a few days ago, I was in Joshua Tree National Park with my family. There, the light makes all the difference. There, the light dictates, frames, and tells the story. Harsh. Gentle. Soft. Cool. Warm. At dawn and dusk, the shadows stretch and imprint.

There too, the heavens feel domed, but with a sky that stretches over and beyond all the horizons. In the early morning light, the landscape is suspended gently by the endless blue sky.

And silence. There is the occasional drone of an airplane. The crunch of stone beneath our feet. The echo of a human voice—maybe a climber or hiker, somewhere beyond our sight. And then, there is nothing. Nothing but the rushing of those noises and voices that clamor in our minds, as if they are spooked by the stillness. One must grow accustomed to the silence.

While driving, we saw a coyote standing by the side of the road. Literally, just standing. We stopped the car. I've seen many coyotes. But always from a distance. Always skittish, running away from any scent of humans. This one was young. And was, apparently, victim of the National Park syndrome: people throw food to animals, animals begin to rely on food handouts, animals grow accustomed to humans and grow less afraid. I was sad, watching as the pup came to our car door. Wanting to chase him away, and to scold him, "Please don't do this. Please. When you do this, you are not a coyote anymore." He stood still, his eyes waiting? Pleading? Resigned?

Perhaps he reminded me of someone I knew, the younger Terry, ever so eager for adulation and handouts, willing to give up his identity for them.

Paying attention, the only game in town

I love mornings in the desert. They are cool, in a way that tells you that this is the respite, the time for relief. The sky is clear. Rarely is there any fog or cloud cover. The treeless hillsides and mountains create a distinct delineation against the sky. This time of year, a khaki brown with the sky a light blue. There is no movement. The picture is stillness. In the foreground a Joshua tree. The sun is not yet harsh.

I have been promising myself time and again to go around some day, unarmed with clubs and carrying no balls, for the express purpose of seeing and enjoying in detail the beauties of the links. There are some woods fringing portions of the course most tempting to explore, woods in which I get glimpses of lovable things, and a wealth of color which, for its very loveliness, I forgive for hiding my sliced ball. . . . There is a great breezy hill bespattered with humble plants, to traverse the broad back of which almost tempts to slice and to pull. A thick boscage, too, whereon the four seasons play a quartet on the theme of green, and every sun-lit day composes a symphony beautiful to behold. And there are nooks, and corners, and knolls, and sloping lawns on which the elfish shadows dance. . . . What is it these things say? Whither do they beckon? What do they reveal? I seem to be listening to some cosmic obligato the while I play; a great and unheard melody swelling from the great heart of Nature. Every golfer knows something of this.

The music is coming from our living room. It is Beatles, "All you need is love." Zach is dancing, a spirited bounce, oblivious to all else. "It's generally only after you've put a few hundred thousand miles or so on the chassis that you are unself-conscious enough to really let go". Thank God he doesn't know this. He sings along at the top of seven-year-old lungs.

He is honoring the day.

He is alive.

Notes

A Note to the Reader
Pablo Casals, *Joys and Sorrows*, as told by Albert E. Kahn. California: Touchstone, 1974.

Czeslaw Milosz, "Gift," in *New and Collected Poems 1931-2001*, translated by Robert Hass, New York: HarperCollins, 2003.

Learning the Big Leaf Dance
Antoine de Saint Exupéry, *The Little Prince*, translated by Richard Howard, New York: Harvest Books edition, 2000.

Mary Oliver, "Gratitude," in *The Leaf and the Cloud: A Poem*, New York: De Capo, 2001.

Patricia Raybon, *My First White Friend: Confessions on Race, Love and Forgiveness*, New York: Penguin, 1997.

Lynne Twist, *The Soul of Money: Transforming Your Relationships with Money and Life*, New York: W. W. Norton and Co., 2003.

Amazement
Michael Mayne, *Sunrise of Wonder: Letters for the Journey*, New York: HarperCollins, 1995.

Witold Rybczynski, *A Clearing in the Distance: Frederick Law Olmstead and America in the Nineteenth Century*, New York: Scribner, 1999.

Charles Frazier, *Cold Mountain*, New York: Vintage, 1998.

Yann Martel, *The Life of Pi*, Toronto, Canada: Random House, 2001.

Sanctuary

Wayne Muller, *Sabbath: Restoring the Sacred Rhythm of Rest*, New York: Bantam, 1999.

John Mitchell, *The Wildest Place on Earth*, New York: Perseus Books Group, 2002.

Marcia Falk, "Will," in *The Book of Blessings: A New Prayer Book for the Weekdays, the Sabbath and the New Moon*, New York: HarperCollins, 1996.

Stillness

Thomas Merton, "Rainard the Rhinoceros" in *Raids on the Unspeakable,* New York: New Directions, 1966.

Doris Grumbach, *The Presence of Absence*, Thorndike, Maine: G. K. Hall & Company, 1999.

Milan Kundera, *Slowness: A Novel*, New York: HarperCollins, 1996.

Thomas Kelly, *The Eternal Promise*, Richmond, IN: Friends United Press, 1988.

Gretel Ehrlich, *The Solace of Open Spaces*, New York: Penguin Books, 1986.

Grace

Annie Dillard, *Pilgrim at Tinker Creek*, New York: HarperCollins, 1998.

Henri Nouwen, *Lifesigns: Intimacy, Fecundity, & Ecstasy In Christian Perspective*, New York, Doubleday, 1986.

Simone Weil, *Waiting for God*, London: Poutledge & Kegan Paul, 1951.

E. L. Doctorow, *City of God*, New York: Random House, 2000.

Simplicity

Lynne Twist, *The Soul of Money: Transforming Your Relationships with Money and Life*, New York: W. W. Norton and Co., 2003.

Bruce Chatwin, Jan Borm, and Matthew Graves, *Anatomy of Restlessness*, New York: Penguin Books, 1997.

Gretel Ehrlich, *The Solace of Open Spaces*, New York: Penguin Books, 1986.

Resilience

Jean-Dominique Bauby, *The Diving Bell and the Butterfly*, New York: Vintage, 1998.

Friendship

Merle Shain, *Hearts That We Broke Long Ago*, New York: Bantam, 1983.

Eugene Kennedy, *On Being a Friend*, New York: Ballantine, 1986.

Thomas Moore, *Soul Mates,* New York: Harper Collins, 1994.

Nancy Jeffery, *Seattle Times,* 4/18/2000.

James Kavanuagh, "Will You be my Friend?" in *Long Quiet Highway: Waking up in America,* by Natalie Goldberg, New York: Bantam, 1994.

Afterword

Barbara Scott, *The Stations of Still Creek,* San Francisco: Sierra Club Books, 1999.

Most days, you'll find Terry out in his garden. More often than not, ambling between roses and perennials, living by the motto that he loses much who has no aptitude for idleness. Terry lives with his wife Judith, and son Zachary, on Vashon, an island in the Puget Sound, near Seattle, Washington, where "ferry" is the sole mode of travel. Rule of thumb: if you have to go anywhere, don't be in a hurry. And yes, he tolerates the rain, so long as he is able to spend some time each winter on Kauai. He is also a rabid Seattle Mariner baseball fan. And he is unabashedly addicted to golf.

Terry was born and raised in Michigan, making it hard to fully purge the University of Michigan blue and gold. His education was a potpourri safari: from Fort Wayne, Indiana to London, England, to Upland, Indiana, to Pasadena, California. His degrees are in Philosophy and Theology from Taylor University and Fuller Theological Seminary, in case anyone is wondering. Armed with two degrees, and fueled by some latent workaholism, Terry spent the next five years as a youth minister, an intern minister, a personnel director for a missionary organization in Japan, and a public relations officer for a firm working in Uganda, Africa.

It took a divorce to slow him down. A crisis that allowed him to reassess his vocational journey. Like it or not, crossroads of that magnitude make you take notice. The next few years Terry spent as a minister of single adults and small groups at a southern California church. During that time, the seed of change from his earlier crisis had begun to take root. It led to the founding of Christian Focus, an organization that provides seminars around the theme of building healthy relationships—all of which requires heavy doses of grace, personal responsibility, and the emphasis on our need to slow down long enough, to let our souls catch up with our bodies . . .

Plain Living
A Quaker Path to Simplicity

Catherine Whitmire

For centuries Quakers have been living out of a spiritual center in a way of life they call "plain living." Their experiences and wisdom have much to offer anyone seeking greater simplicity today.

ISBN: 1-893732-28-2 / 192 pages / $14.95
SORIN BOOKS

Tickle Your Soul   18,500 sold!
Live Well, Love Much, Laugh Often

Anne Bryan Smollin

Tickle Your Soul enables readers to "wrinkle their faces with smiles" and avoid "drying up their souls like prunes." Captured in a happy blend of psychological and spiritual principles, coupled with anecdotes and folk wisdom, *Tickle Your Soul* delivers joy, health, and wellness.

ISBN: 1-893732-00-2 / 160 pages / $12.95
SORIN BOOKS

This Blessed Mess   29,500 sold!
Finding Hope Amidst Life's Chaos

Patricia H. Livingston

Offering hope and encouragement in the face of life's chaos, Livingston's good-humored stories are sure to resonate with readers. With wit and wisdom, Livingston shares with us her lifetime of taming chaos. She assures us that in the midst of all the "craziness" we can discover the seeds of creativity and hope.

ISBN: 1-893732-15-0 / 144 pages / $12.95
SORIN BOOKS

Secular Sanctity   15,500 sold!
Reflections on Finding God in the Midst of Daily Life

Edward Hays

This wise and practical handbook for seeking the sacred in the secular world offers you 18 challenging essays on finding holiness in such everyday areas of life as hospitality, music, letter writing, work, sacred idleness, and meditation.

ISBN: 0-939516-05-5 / 144 pages / $10.95
FOREST OF PEACE

KEYCODE: F0S01050000